A STEP-PARENT'S

C000154148

KATE RAPHAEL is stepmother to five children, and also has two young children of her own, so she has first-class experience of all the pleasures and problems of a stepfamily. She is Personal Assistant to an Executive Producer, Granada Television, Manchester. She previously taught French. She is also a counsellor for the Stepfamily Association.

Overcoming Common Problems Series

Overcoming Common Problems Series

How to Cope with your Nerves
DR TONY LAKE

How to Cope with Tinnitus and Hearing Loss
DR ROBERT YOUNGSON

How to do What You Want to Do
DR PAUL HAUCK

How to Enjoy Your Old Age
DR B. F. SKINNER AND M. E.
VAUGHAN

How to Love and be Loved
DR PAUL HAUCK

How to Sleep Better
DR PETER TYRER

How to Stand up for Yourself
DR PAUL HAUCK

How to Start a Conversation and Make Friends
DON GABOR

How to Stop Smoking
GEORGE TARGET

Jealousy
DR PAUL HAUCK

Learning to Live with Multiple Sclerosis
DR ROBERT POVEY, ROBIN DOWIE
AND GILLIAN PRETT

Living with Grief
DR TONY LAKE

Living with High Blood Pressure
DR TOM SMITH

Loneliness
DR TONY LAKE

Making Marriage Work
DR PAUL HAUCK

Making the Most of Middle Age
DR BRICE PITT

Making the Most of Yourself
GILL COX AND SHEILA DAINOW

Making Relationships Work
CHRISTINE SANDFORD AND WYN
BEARDSLEY

Meeting People is Fun
How to overcome shyness
DR PHYLLIS SHAW

No More Headaches
LILIAN ROWEN

One Parent Families
DIANA DAVENPORT

Overcoming Tension
DR KENNETH HAMBLY

The Parkinson's Disease Handbook
DR RICHARD GODWIN-AUSTEN

Second Wife, Second Best?
Managing your marriage as a second wife
GLYNNIS WALKER

Self-Help for your Arthritis
EDNA PEMBLE

The Sex Atlas
DR ERWIN HAEBERLE

Six Weeks to a Healthy Back
ALEXANDER MELLEBY

Solving your Personal Problems
PETER HONEY

A Step-Parent's Handbook
KATE RAPHAEL

Stress and your Stomach
DR VERNON COLEMAN

Overcoming Common Problems Series

Overcoming Common Problems

A STEP-PARENT'S HANDBOOK

Kate Raphael

SHELDON PRESS
LONDON

First published in Great
Britain in 1986 by
Sheldon Press, SPCK, Marylebone Road,
London NW1 4DU

British Library Cataloguing in Publication Data

Raphael, Kate
  A step-parent's handbook.——(Overcoming common problems)
  1. Stepparents —— Psychology
  I. Title   II. Series
  306.8'74   HQ759.92

  ISBN 0-85969-508-5
  ISBN 0-85969-509-3 Pbk

Typeset by Deltaype, Ellesmere Port
Printed in Great Britain by
Richard Clay (The Chaucer Press) Ltd,
Bungay, Suffolk.

Contents

1
Statistics Aside . . .

There's something curious happening to the 'Mummy, Daddy, Janet and John' family we grew up with in the picture books. Janet and John are still there – but what about Mummy and Daddy?

This book is designed to shed some light on the emotional and practical aspects of joining families and living happily within them, and not concerned with examining statistics. Nevertheless, there is one statistic that cannot be ignored here: the one and a half million children affected by divorce every year. And the number isn't static; it is growing. In real terms, this means that the one in three casualty rate for first marriages and the two in three rate for second marriages are not just figures one reads about: they refer to you and me, our families and friends. In reading this book your main interest may be in restructuring your own family, or in adjusting to see your children less often during a period of separation or divorce. You may want to gain a little insight into the business of introducing your family to a new partner, or into making it easier for partners and their families to merge happily and successfully.

Bereavement also leaves gaps in families. On paper, we are set to enjoy a longer life, yet a great number of young and middle-aged people die leaving children. With luck, a widow or widower will meet someone else hoping to form a permanent relationship which will provide a happy environment for one family or more.

Single parents who meet partners may be surprised and pleased to find a companion to share the joys and responsibilities of bringing up children, especially if they embarked on parent-hood in circumstances that were less than ideal. Taking all the different backgrounds into consideration, it comes as no surprise that forming a relationship with someone who is already a parent is a strong possibility.

The role of women in stepfamilies deserves special consider-ation. Why? Because in many cases it is a woman who is the central figure in the family. Most children remain with their mother after the parents' divorce, which means that she is the linchpin of the group. But there is a 'shadow' job too: a father may remarry or have a long-term relationship, in which case another woman will have to get to know his children. Her influence and her attitude to her partner's offspring will affect their morale a great deal. In spite of all the difficulties that may be involved, if you are in this position it is worth making an extra effort, even if you have never really had much to do with children before. The politics of divorce are notoriously divisive. If only the two women in the 'mother' roles could get together: there would be everything to gain, with some hope of security and continuity for the family in question. Unfortunately, too many women are left to get on with it by themselves. They undertake to look after children they don't know, often in an atmosphere suffused with antagonism, and when panic, resentment and confusion set in, they give up – which in many cases is quite understandable. What could have been fruitful relationships never have a chance to get off the ground – and it can all end in tears, with adults and children alike feeling bruised and guilty. Our social mythology seems to dictate that all women, regardless of personality, taste and ability, have a natural mothering instinct. If such an instinct comes hard enough where one's own children are concerned, what are the chances of it blossoming overnight with children one doesn't even know?

Step-parenthood, however, is not the exclusive preserve of women. Men are emerging from being the passive – by which I mean merely the breadwinning – force in the family and making their feelings about children known. They are frequently the ones who have to carve a place for themselves in a woman partner's family. How do they set about it? What works, and what doesn't? And what is it like for a man to move into his partner's family and see his own children only occasionally or infrequently?

Then there are the 'double' families: joint ventures formed where partners meet and eventually make a home together, hoping that their two sets of offspring will co-exist happily. It has been said to me that the initial view is of a glorious, brightly-coloured canvas: a fantasy picture of two happy, fulfilled adults surrounded by various equally happy, fulfilled youngsters. That, in short, is the ideal. The portrait painters who hope to attain this sometimes have to start with a large and complicated jigsaw, making the best of the pieces they've got!

It is quite impossible to try to set out any kind of blueprint because the individuals, like the situations, vary so widely. Parents, partners or children – we all fear what we do not know. We all fear what is alien to us when there seem to be no clear-cut rules for guidance. It is hoped that the small amount of information this book contains will help someone, somewhere. The society we live in is closely geared to the gathering and dissemination of information, providing access to help of practically every kind, whether by letter, telephone or computer. Sit in a doctor's surgery and you will see different kinds of posters spelling out ways of obtaining help and advice, some dealing with matters that are strictly medical, others covering a wider subject area. There is, so it appears, a phone number for just about everything – so what about step-parents and their families? Since 1983 there has been an association dealing with all aspects of the situation. Called STEPFAMILY (The National Stepfamily Association), it is a recognized charity. Members receive a regular newsletter and are put in touch with individuals and families in a similar position; they are also supplied with news of books, broadcasts and forthcoming events of interest to step-parents and their children. The main benefit of joining, of course, is the knowledge that as a member of a stepfamily one needn't be alone.

STEPFAMILY (The National Stepfamily Association),
Ross Street Community Centre,
Ross Street,
Cambridge
CB2 3BS

Membership is £5 per annum at time of going to press. Send a stamped adressed envelope for a copy of their newsletter, or telephone 0223-215370 for further information.

Many other counselling services do an excellent job, and there is no reason why a parent, partner or child shouldn't get in touch with a local clergyman, the local social services, Samaritans or Citizens' Advice Bureau. The admirable Marriage Guidance Council takes an interest in stepfamilies, too. Yet all these established services already carry a heavy burden, and they may not be able to provide immediate access to a suitably trained or experienced counsellor. Statistics aside, regrouping families need help and encouragement. It is tragic to think that an already fragile relationship or second marriage may be in peril and about to end in crisis because help and information were not available when they were needed.

One last thought, before stepfamily matters come under closer examination. My own eldest stepdaughter, in her twenties, once told a group of neighbouring children who were visiting her house that it was time they left, as she was about to go and see her dad. She also mentioned that she had a stepmother. 'Ooh!' the kids exclaimed, their eyes shining. 'Is she wicked?!' Stepfamilies may represent the relationship of the Eighties as there are now so many of us involved – yet it is clear that we 'wicked' step-parents still have a long way to go!

2

What is a Step-Parent?

A step-parent is an adult who shares his/her life with a parent. By this I mean someone who sees his/her partner's children at weekends or holiday time, or someone who has the partner and children with him/her permanently – on the face of it, just like an 'ordinary' family. Some adult partners may not meet the children, but it is worth bearing in mind that circumstances can – and do – change. Consider yourself a potential step-parent if you spend your time with a person who has children. Should you start coming into regular contact with the family this small but significant detail will help a great deal.

There is really no step-parent 'type': virtually anyone who meets and becomes attracted to a parent wishing to form a long-term relationship can be considered a candidate. Historically speaking, we have not always been as attached to our children as we are now; the lifelong bond between parent and child is a relatively recent development, enhanced now that a large family is no longer considered a mandatory part of a lasting, sexually active marriage. Since contraception became available to the masses most of us have become used to thinking in terms of limiting the number of children we have and of enjoying a permanent bond with them; we are no longer forced to leave the last few for adoption or to send others out to work. Throw divorce or bereavement into this firmer structure, and chaos will ensue. Yet the parental bond remains as firm. And after a divorce, parents are often disturbed by the altered form of contact they are expected to have with their children. 'Access' is seldom what the term implies but just a makeshift arrangement which is designed to fulfil the letter of the law and fills the non-custodial parent with gloom. Whatever the circumstances, whether it's a question of sharing full parental responsibilities or doing one's best at weekends and in the holidays, a partner will find it hard to make his/her place in the family.

What about you?

A woman reading this could be involved with a family man, even at a relatively young age: today it is not invariably the middle-aged 'spinster' who ends up caring for a stepfamily. You may be thinking of joining a family; or you may already be in their midst, pausing only now to wonder what it all entails.

A man reading this book could also be considering joining a family and sharing the responsibilities generally allotted to the mother. He could find it slightly easier to assume a father's role as opposed to a mother's. While it is entirely up to the family concerned to decide who does what, a man is unlikely to encounter problems as severe as those faced by a female partner about to take on another woman's child(ren).

Where are you up to?

First, what may seem a rather personal question: are you married? Have you therefore already passed 'go', and do you now face the future complete with your partner's (and perhaps your own) family in residence? If so, your interest in this book may be concentrated in certain key areas. You may, let us say, want to know more about coping with weekends, or how best to prepare for certain eventualities, such as when a stepchild suddenly asks to come and live with you. If you are already married, then there is no time for theory: you may never have had a 'trying-out' period, in any case, and it is possible that a previous marriage and experience of family life have taught you much of what you need to know – even if it's what to avoid! If you are already married but were previously childless, then it is hoped that some of the topics dealt with in this book will be of interest to you.

For those not yet legally married to a parent but considering taking that step, there is much to think about. It would be marvellous if all potential difficulties could be unravelled before the decision was made to marry or do the deed, but things aren't always that easy. There is a great deal to be said for living with your partner, getting to know him/her and the children involved beforehand, on whatever basis you may see them. I lived with my partner for some years before we married, and during that time the situation changed considerably, converting me from a 'weekend' stepmother to a full-time one. I am very glad, in retrospect, to have had this period, which I now look back on as a form of on-the-job training: the theory content was almost negligible, the practical work plentiful and the initiative course powerful! Had I, at the time, been able to buy a widely available paperback, talk with or attend a group consisting of other men and women in the same situation, I am sure I would have learned faster. And I would not perhaps have been quite so taken aback by all that was expected of me.

That period of romantic progress which bears the quaint name of courtship and is depicted in so many novels and films is virtually unknown to the step-parent, whether he/she is a parent or not. As for us, we certainly did not have the luxury of one: my suitor was not always in a position to whisk me away for an intimate weekend, and even as newly-weds we were unable to lock the doors and concentrate on being Alone Together. This has been pointed out to me on more than one occasion. I listen with good humour to accounts of how some of my contemporaries, now enjoying live-in or wedded bliss, conducted the early stages of their relationships and it becomes clear that I am required to state why I appear not to have experienced the same things. Well, just try conducting a courtship in the thick of family life and see how far you get! Try planning a honeymoon, for instance: I think some of the glamour disappears when it comes to the nitty-gritty of deciding who's going to look after the children. How many romantic dinners-for-two get knocked on the head because children turn up unexpectedly or can't be found babysitters? And what chance have you got, as a mum or dad, of impressing your lover when two or three adolescents have already had a good laugh at the spectacle of you dressing up for an evening out?

It isn't always possible to think out all the likely problems before one marries. Partners taking the plunge for a second time frequently dispense with the traditional courtship period: often, there are few practical reasons why they should wait. Yet in ideal circumstances how the two partners individually and together think of their children and how they are going to manage life with a husband's, wife's or 'joint' family is something that calls for a great deal of thought and discussion. If nothing else, some serious consideration beforehand would help to avoid the inevitable feeling of 'You didn't tell me' or 'I didn't expect this'.

What do you want?

Whether you are a potential or actual stepmother/stepfather, what are your expectations? Are you anticipating few problems, hoping life with your partner and family will go smoothly? Or do you dread the whole business, secretly welcoming opinions which would have you believe that the children really aren't your responsibility? It's worth looking at a step-parent's motivation: which simply means trying to decide, with no excuses, whether or not you are really willing.

See how you react to these questions in broad terms of a 'yes' or 'no' answer:

When thinking about your future, do you tend to think in terms of *you and your partner*?

Do you think your partner thinks of the future in much the same way?

Do your partner's children appear in the picture, but only in the background?

Are you reluctant to think of your partner's children sharing some or all of your time?

If the children became a permanent part of your lives, do you think this should be on *your* terms?

In a life shared with a partner and children, would you hope to impose certain conditions, such as arranging a number of regular evenings out or alone together/weekends or holidays away or alone together?

In a disagreement involving the whole family, should your partner support *you* rather than the children?

8

If you have three or more 'yes' answers, you are to be congratulated on your frankness – but you could be in for a hard time. You could disregard most of the questions because, on the face of it, there is almost nil involvement with the children. This often seems to be the case when there are scant access arrangements, with the absent parent and children hardly meeting. Yet this could turn out to be, in a rather old-fashioned phrase, something of a snare and a delusion, because things can change with breathtaking speed, suddenly turning you into an active figure in the family whether you felt like it or not. If you haven't prepared yourself mentally for anything like this, it will be very hard to digest.

No one expects an overnight conversion from ordinary mortal to winged saint, but it cannot be denied that living with a partner and children, whether at weekends or permanently, calls for a higher degree of willingness than usual to put yourself at the back of the queue. Having said that, it would be quite wrong to assume that the ideal step-parent is a mere doormat. You need a firm belief in yourself and your abilities; but this is best used as reserve strength, rather than as a battering ram to get your own way.

If you really can't see yourself as part of a group rather than one of a couple enjoying the privacy and other 'perks' such a relationship brings, then there are definitely hard knocks ahead. It isn't good enough, if you have serious reservations now, to say, too late: 'I didn't think your family were more important than me!' In a stepfamily, importance is not the pecking order you might imagine, and seeking your place in any kind of hierarchy, particularly the hypothetical one of the partner's affections, is non-productive. Everyone is important in a stepfamily: the children in one way and the adults in another.

Many people who consider marrying a partner with children are quite unaware of what this involves. There is a great temptation to diminish the significance of the family as a whole, not because the children are disliked by a partner or neglected by a parent but because attention is often paid to the couple making their way in the world rather than to the group as a whole. A friend or relative may hasten to assure a potential step-parent, especially a childless one, that 'All the children live with their mother . . . you'll never see them'; whereas if only that person had thought through that remark he/she would add: 'But, you never know, they might one day prefer to live with you.' This would be more honest, and would help prepare everyone for such an eventuality.

A friend whose experience of life's problems and pleasures alike is rich and varied once said to me when I confronted her with yet another moan about my stepchildren: 'Demand less. Accept more.' That, in a nutshell, is what being a step-parent is all about. Young or not so young, intellectual or otherwise, articulate or the reverse, skilled or unskilled, step-parents come in every variety. The main attribute dictating success or failure is willingness: whatever your degree of involvement, the family cannot learn to accept you and coexist happily with you if you simply refuse to accept them.

3

Same Again?

We are all having to rethink the way we picture today's family. Times have changed, and whereas twenty or thirty years ago the lone parent could be regarded as slightly exceptional, this is no longer so today. It is a cue to everyone to stop looking even vaguely surprised and to get on with accepting and helping the new status quo, whether it be one parent in sole charge, parent plus new partner in total or partial charge of the children or two single parents getting together in the hope of merging their families successfully. There is a strong tendency to assume that just because one remarries it will be 'business as usual' from the day after the honeymoon, with new 'mothers' slipping easily into the role of domestic supervisor and new 'fathers' being responsible for family finance and discipline – all very neat and tidy.

It isn't just the world in general, one's friends and family, who hope that a lone mother/father will find a mate and co-worker to help with the children: bereaved or divorced parents often go through a very painful time where they would almost snatch the first opportunity of re-creating the complete family life they appear to have lost. My own husband, for example, has described to me his feeling of wishing above all to slip back into the 'husband-and-father' way of life once the dust appeared to have settled following his divorce. He did indeed find family life again – but not until some eight years later. He lived through that lonely time, resisting the temptation he felt so keenly to 'propose to practically the first decent girl I met, just to settle down again'. He did not live like a hermit but got back into the way of having an independent social life and achieved, with difficulty, some sort of balance with his children. He began to think very carefully about 'settling down' again – and who wouldn't, with five children to consider?

People can and do take the plunge once the worst is over; hence the high number of second and subsequent marriages, many of which involve children. But concern enters the picture when it is realized how fragile those relationships can be. In Britain, one in three marriages fails for first-timers; two in three for older hands. What goes wrong? I wish I knew how to isolate all the problems so that we could all be warned! Are expectations any lower, just because a man or woman has been married before? Or is there any less romance? Are we all just as ready to fall helplessly in love without considering whether the whole gang – children, grandparents and so on – will take to our new partner?

I think we all do fall in love fairly helplessly. We do tend to have high expectations of a second (or subsequent) marriage, welcoming the chance to wipe the slate clean and get it right this time. As if the business of getting to know and trust another adult weren't complicated enough, there's a family to think about. When it's just a one-to-one adult relationship we can, if it all ends in tears, recover and learn from it. In time we come to accept that it wasn't the right combination, that he or she wasn't the right person, that we ourselves were too trusting, not open enough or whatever. But how do you cope when it's not just you but a family which might suffer from a failed attempt?

There is an argument for having a completely separate social life, for conducting one's affairs outside the home, having a boyfriend/girlfriend who doesn't come into contact with the children so that friction is avoided. Fine in theory – but has anyone tried it? If so, what happens? My guess is that in return for a short period of adult companionship there are niggling doubts and insufficiencies. It can be complicated, going out with a partner who isn't really 'declared' to one's children. Besides, children get to know, and dislike having any kind of wool pulled over their eyes. One of my stepchildren has told me she knew perfectly well if Daddy was going out with a girlfriend. She would then turn up coincidentally, whereupon he would make a great point of saying what a delightful surprise it was that they could all spend the day together. Or else the observant family would witness Daddy bidding them a hasty goodbye because they knew very well he was going to go home and change – to take 'her' out. And we're looking at a man who at that point didn't even have the family under his roof!

And what happens if the couple are making steady progress, with much catching up to do on the part of the children? It isn't easy, surely, to break the news that you're going to get married again to a barely prepared audience. Some years ago I was teaching in a boarding school, the kind of place where the staff get to know the pupils very well. As the joyful pupils were running out of my class, one of them appeared to lag behind. She looked very down that day – a Monday – and when she told me what was in a letter she'd received that morning, I knew why. 'My dad got married again on Saturday,' she said – and it was a long time until the next weekend out or main holiday. That little girl had a lot of worrying to do.

Why 'same again' won't work

As human beings capable of thought, we all know that second marriages, whatever their background, are likely to be the same as first ones. Here, then, is the problem: while we know intellectually that we cannot expect the same qualities from a second marriage, we all, rather covertly, have very similar *emotional* expectations. Just like the divorced or bereaved man who feels dreadfully lonely and wishes he could get back into a domestic life full of comfort and companionship, we all feel the loss when our life-style has been torn from us, regardless of the parts of it which may have been practically intolerable. Paying lip-service to the fact that next time round it has to be different but hoping against hope that we're going to be back in a warm, friendly, romantic partnership with the family in sweet order is not good enough.

The new partnership: from the woman's point of view

Here I shall discuss women as mothers. The end of one partnership has been sealed, and another is either on the horizon or in existence. Why shouldn't it resemble the first?

● You may have known what it is like to assume the

13

responsibilities of the whole family while bereaved of or separated from your previous partner. Do you want to hand things over unconditionally to a new partner? You may have known incidents which terrorized you or filled you with despair – but, for good or ill, you have come through them and are possibly a stronger person because of them. You are now going to have to look at the issue of partnership, especially in terms of handling your children, in a completely new light.

- Leading on from that aspect of things, there is very possibly the children's natural father to consider. This can lead to a number of problems in the case of an acrimonious divorce, and it raises different issues if the parting of the ways was a reasonably civilized one. It could be that the most indifferent of natural fathers will suddenly express a fresh interest in his children once a new male partner appears on the scene. Even if this is not the case, you will have to juggle a father and a partner somehow – all very different from the time you were just one half of a couple.

- Since the heady days of marrying for the first time a great deal has happened. Even if it now looks as though the worst is over, with the nastiness and upheaval of divorce or the grief of bereavement almost at an end, you will still be surprised at the conflicting emotions you experience. On the face of it, you may have what you hoped for: your family still intact, your self-respect *and* a new partner. But to quote a friend speaking of her second marriage with a new husband and two small children to care for: 'I did a lot of crying – all round the house and not just at night.'

- There are financial and very practical problems to be resolved at the outset of a new partnership, some of which are bound to involve raking over the coals of your previous marriage. (Hardly the stuff of which dreams are made, when you have to thrash out with your new man how you will both keep a roof over the family's head!)

- Your children are the most tangible reminder of your last

marriage. In some cases, this can prove almost too much to bear: consider the feelings of a woman who is deeply relieved to be away from her ex-husband and who, daily, cares for his living image. Highly idealized 'family life' is put on a pedestal, and we are made to feel guilty if this state of affairs is not allowed to continue. But it does not have to be duplicated, does it? There can be as much safely and security as you can make but with new ingredients added which will more than substitute for unwelcome reminders of the unhappy periods of the past.

Women, especially those who have children, may need the least reminding that a second or subsequent marriage cannot be like the first. Once they have dealt with the practicalities of the family they become sharply aware of this, and though they may welcome a male partner with whom to share domestic respon-sibilities as well as love and friendship, they are unlikely to want to slip back into the ways of the past.

The new partnership: for fathers

It has finally happened: you are being offered another chance to be part of a couple again and find that elusive 'family' way of life. But don't settle back too comfortably: it's seat-belt time for the proverbial bumpy ride! And here are the reasons why:

- Like your ex-partner you too will have evolved, for good or ill, through the difficulties you have experienced and still are experiencing, perhaps. For all its familiarity you may not genuinely care for your 'old' way of life, even if you were able to return to it. The pain has forced progress, which is important – don't throw it away.

- Your new partner may be very unlike your previous spouse in a variety of ways. She may be younger than you, and childless: quite different from the girl you once married and who grew with you into parenthood. Alternatively, she may have children of her own – so that *you* have a new family to get used to. This can be hard, especially if you see your own children only intermittently.

15

But what happens to the kind of man who *does* hope life will go on in the same way as before?

Jean-Michel was an eminent surgeon who lived for his work. When his wife died, he was lost: he no longer had a mother for his children or a loyal, competent colleague (his wife had been a doctor too). Everyone was thrilled when two years later he met and married a most attractive and charming young woman. She was young enough to qualify as a friend, rather than a mother, to his two teenage children, and everyone predicted happiness all round.

Jean-Michel certainly was happy; he had a wife again: a companion and lover. His son was pleased because, for purely selfish reasons, he could now count Dad as 'off his back'. To this young man, who was wishing to study away from home and travel abroad, a stepmother seemed a boon. But Jean-Michel's daughter felt differently. She had become very important to her father during his widowerhood and although his insistence that she should now be 'liberated' from her former household duties to achieve the all-important entry into university was fine in theory, it caused anguish in practice. What her father had perceived as a blessing she felt as a kick in the teeth.

Jean-Michel simply wanted life to continue as before – with his new wife running the household. He probably knew perfectly well that he would be unable to reproduce the same form of family life that he had enjoyed during his first marriage, but it didn't stop him from expecting it. And as he tended to be a man of few words, not given to the discussion of deep personal matters, neither his wife nor his daughter had a chance to confide in him; indeed, the very prospect of such a thing made him feel vulnerable, as if the two women were asking him to take sides. And rather than do that he retreated into his work. It wasn't as if he was uncaring and insensitive – he was most concerned about them both – but he just expected life to continue as it had before: without fuss. Although outwardly his second marriage was a happy one his new wife felt she had paid dearly, with an uphill struggle lasting many years, to marry the man she loved.

So the new relationship is unlikely to be the same as the previous one. And it is worth while trying to use the very differences you initially find so hard to deal with as positive signs of change and development rather than awkward stumbling-blocks. If you have a new childless partner, do try to consider her feelings: your children, much as you love them, are unfamiliar territory to her. They may even welcome your new start, but it is unlikely that they will manifest rapture from the moment they set eyes on her.

The new partnership: for children

It is terribly easy to get involved in deep thought and discussion about the adults' place in new partnerships, pondering the suitability of one life-style or another, one home or another, one point of view or another. It is terribly easy to overlook *children*.

They are creatures of habit, far more so than adults are. You have only to think of the toddler's insistence on the same bedtime routine every night, come what may: if the teeth-cleaning, last trip to the loo, getting into bed and bedtime story do not follow a prescribed sequence, there can be trouble! Because of this they tend to cling to 'old' ways of doing things and make a point of insisting on doing so even if they are really too grown-up to appear to need it. Their rigidity over meals, time to watch television, small details related to going out (or not) or virtually any other thing connected with family life you may care to mention can make life very hard indeed for two adults trying to find their feet in a new partnership. Such stubbornness can appear dog-in-the-mangerish, which is a neat and unassailable way of making the new adult partner feel excluded.

What such slavishness conceals is perhaps profound doubt and insecurity. We all know, incidentally, that to be insecure is no longer unfashionable: all the closet teddybear huggers can now 'come out' since it is no longer a crime to own up to feeling adrift. Children can entertain some fairly wild imaginings when their parent (or parents) remarries. My own stepchildren admit that their greatest fear was that their divorcing parents would *both* exit and find new partners with whom they would then have more babies. They now know this was unlikely – but tell that to five children whose world seemingly falls apart. At the time each of their parents was young enough to consider having another family, although this was hard to imagine, especially given the lengthy process of getting divorced and attempting to settle the question of custody with such a large number of children involved. Nevertheless, there must have been many dark nights when the children, from the eldest downwards, prayed they wouldn't wake up to find that either their mother or their father had married again and was having further offspring. They were quite sure that in the event of such a thing happening they would find themselves in some kind of limbo, belonging to neither Mummy nor Daddy. Small wonder that in the face of change they clung steadfastly to some of their old way of life: it was just about all they had.

The new partnership: for partners

By this I mean those men and women who marry parents. For some it may not be a second marriage but a first, to an individual who has done it all before. This makes for some strange conflicts of expectation: it's hard to reconcile the inevitable romance of one's first marriage with the slightly more down-to-earth requirements of a second. Even the actual business of getting married can cause problems – take my own case. Why was I not doing it in style, with the religious ceremony, white dress, beribboned cars and ruinously expensive reception, followed by a once-in-a-lifetime honeymoon and leaving behind four perfectly matched bridesmaids? A good question: I was marrying a divorced man of a different faith from mine – and with five children. The differing faiths kissed goodbye to the church (or synagogue) wedding, and it is difficult to manoeuvre oneself in and out of a register office in the required time in full bridal regalia. Quite apart from these considerations, my husband had been married before, and with the full ceremonial: superstition probably warned him not to try that again! And then there's the honeymoon. In our case, we had been living together for some time and already had one of the five children with us permanently. Not easy to organize a romantic 'away-from-it-all' holiday – unless, of course, we made it a threesome. I can see a young woman who takes on a man with children coming in for a considerable amount of flak when trying to decide how best to organize the big day. The bride's mother may shed tears over not being able to arrange the perfect replica of the most recent royal wedding, but she would be well advised to compromise and abide by the couple's wishes. Having got over the actual business of matrimony (or arrived at a decision to live together), what should the new partner bear in mind?

- The tangible reminders of your wife or husband's first marriage, namely the children. You are not taking on just an individual; it's a real 'package' which must be accepted in its entirety. Unfortunately you can't have the individual man or woman without the family, so these will be around either full time (as is often the case where a male partner is concerned) or part time (in the case of a stepmother).

- Invisible reminders of the first marriage, such as inevitable references to things the couple did (or didn't do), memories of family activities, holidays and so forth, along with habits formed during that first partnership.

Arlette was unmarried and childless when she met her husband, a charming, intelligent man with three daughters. They were still quite young when their father remarried, and on the face of it all was set to go well. Profound relief was expressed on all sides that a lone father had found a new wife – and weren't the little girls fortunate to have a 'new mummy'? Indeed they were, but things weren't quite so simple as that. Arlette found herself up against ingrained family tradition at every turn, starting with the house where they lived. Having lunch with the family one day, I was slightly bewildered to note the frost which seemed to settle on the table once the main course had been dealt with. (In those days I was not a stepmother but a mere student.) The subject of controversy was the pudding: Arlette was fond of desserts and planned to serve something special as there was a guest. 'The girls' had never had 'pudding' after meals, not to mention a hot dessert, and were definitely not entertaining the idea, guest or no. It was such a small matter, yet it cast quite a cloud over the end of the meal, with the girls filing out solemnly

19

watched by their dismayed but silent father and annoyed stepmother.

The minute details of family life – all the potential minefields of meals and bedtimes, help in the house and general adaptation to the new partner or group – will be discussed later, but perhaps the above example will at least serve to illustrate how strong feelings can be over something that many adults may consider trivial.

The new partnership: for bystanders

'Bystanders' may seem a peculiar term and one that doesn't quite describe the close relatives of parents and step-parents, but I am using it here to refer to all those who witness their relative or friend embarking on this new way of life. Don't think that the parent, step-parent and children are the only ones with work to do!

Have you ever noticed the relief – and haste – with which the whole family gets 'filed away' once a previously lone parent (or pair of lone parents) finds a partner and decides either to live with that partner or remarry? Thank heavens John (or Mary) has found someone else to help him out and keep him company – or even to give him another chance, a fresh start, an opportunity for further children. What a relief! We can stop worrying about John and put him in the 'ordinary families' drawer – after all, there are all the conventional components, aren't there? On the face of it there are two adults and children, just like in any other family.

This, however, is where the similarity ends. In fact, just as you hoped that your friend or relative's problems were over, it will probably seem as if they are only just starting. Your friend, far from hitting the emotional jackpot, with the dream of no more loneliness realized, finds there is a whole new jungle out there, which you will have to come to terms with, too.

It can be very hard for bystanders: how far can loyalty stretch? Can you take on board someone's new partner with sincerity, giving the couple the assistance they need, or do you feel awkward because of your closeness to your friend's previous spouse? How do you counter remarks made by the children, who are somewhat bewildered and tend to pass on certain remarks made by their currently absent parent? If you have reservations about the new partner, how do you come to terms with them – and what if you're convinced that the new regime won't work? As the friend/relative of either a potential step-parent or a parent about to remarry you may wield more power than you realize.

Michael is a stepfather who before his marriage was single and childless. Of his friends'/relatives' reactions to the scheme, he says:

> I found it hard at times because I cared about my friends and family and hoped they would give me good advice. When I told them of my plans I was shocked and hurt by their reaction, mainly because I do care about these people – enough to want to talk it over with them. I hadn't bargained for the rejection I would feel . . . but the few who have supported me have done so without reservation. That has made all the difference in the world.

The areas in which friends and relatives can exert maximum influence – whether positive or negative – will be discussed later (see Chapter 6). Once the 'new' stepfamily has been created, don't write it off: a good listening ear and a few objective suggestions can sometimes work miracles.

If it's not 'same again', what is it?

Stepfamilies don't fall easily into categories, and appear to defy most conventional attempts to identify them. The individuals concerned do not belong to one nuclear family, and neither do they fall into a 'biological family' slot. Broadly speaking, they are what I prefer to call 'restructured' families: groups of people who have emerged from the trauma of divorce or bereavement. The adults acquire new partners, while the children often acquire siblings who are younger, older or their contemporaries. To try for convenience' sake to pigeon-hole such groups by labelling their members as 'new mums', 'new dads' or – perhaps even worse – 'new brothers and sisters' is to do them a disservice. The social trends which create stepfamilies are increasingly strong in our world: fragmented families – and the happier sequel of restructured ones – are here to stay. It is highly unfortunate that the title of stepmother and stepfather should bear such unhappy associations, the legacy of centuries of ignorance and super- stition. But unless we resort to fanciful name-changes (some quite witty, others frankly whimsical), these are the only terms we've got. 'Stepmother' and 'stepfather' should be regarded as no more than identification tags helpful when making those first, necessary introductions. After that, the stepfamily is just what its members and supporters make of it.

Restructuring is a new kind of family life which we all, whether participants or bystanders, must accept. If we can liberate ourselves sufficiently to grasp the fact that a fragmented family can be restructured successfully without reverting to 'Mum, Dad and the children', we shall be one important step nearer to perceiving some of the basic difficulties of such rebuilding programmes – and to overcoming them.

4

A Woman's Place . . .?

In Victorian days, the widow struggling to raise her family in dire yet genteel poverty made a touching picture. The more fortunate widower, on the other hand, may have been introduced to a willing soul who agreed to help him with his (doubtless vast) family. The likely candidate would be the poorest, plainest daughter of a clergyman or respectable tradesman. Lacking the beauty of the town belle or the fortune of the mill-owner's daughter and possibly not equipped with a great deal of education, she could expect to do far worse than provide a home for Mr Right – and all the little Rights!

A woman taking on a man and his offspring in the 1980s is unlikely to belong to this unhappy breed of females on the lookout for a husband. She is no latter-day member of the famous 'fishing fleet' shipped out a century ago to the colonies in search of lonely and eligible bachelors (or destined to make do with family men if that is all they could get). Today a woman's place is where she chooses, and marriage into a stepfamily in no way implies that she could hope for little else.

This chapter is directed for the most part at the previously single, childless woman who takes on a man and his family for some or all of the time. She is the 'shadow mother' whose responsibilities at the outset may not be very clear. If a man's children are living permanently with his former wife, he and his new partner may seem to have little involvement with them; but even if this is so the quality of that involvement counts for a great deal. And, as I have stated on numerous occasions, the nature of your involvement with the children may well change: what starts as something that is strictly limited can become quite the reverse. Once children see that their father has a companion, someone who appears willing to help look after them or at the very least to help him provide a possible home, anything can happen.

So where, in this confusing outlook, does a 'woman's place' lie? It could be in the background, especially in the case of a comparatively new relationship, or more in the forefront as the two partners begin to feel more at ease with each other. A realist will tell you that as a stepmother your place is invariably in the wrong – and there is some truth in that, too!

It is most important to be prepared to work hard at your contact with the children, even if at first you shrink from the prospect. And a woman unused to dealing with someone else's family would surely be superhuman if she didn't feel even faintly reluctant.

That 'weekend' feeling

Let's start with the woman whose relationship with her partner is yet to reach the stage where her participation at every 'family' weekend is asked for. Here it is probably most practical for her to meet the family occasionally, with minimal pressure being put on the children to accept their father's girlfriend as a permanent fixture. This occasional contact will make sure that the children know whom their father is seeing in his spare time and what she is like, thus stemming any fears before they start and perhaps paving the way to further meetings. If the relationship progresses, the children will not suffer from having anything 'sprung' on them; if it doesn't, they are unlikely to suffer too much disappointment either. This tactic also, and quite importantly, prevents any guilt from being heaped upon their heads: children in such a situation shouldn't be made to feel that if Dad's girlfriend takes off it is in any way their fault. (This is despite the kind of propaganda so often displayed in feature films, where we see the little darlings conspiring to get rid of a potential stepmother!)

What about the woman whose relationship with her partner is somewhat more stable? Weekends with the family are on the horizon: a few may have taken place already. One thing is certain: she will have to rearrange her customary way of life so as to accommodate her partner's children. After the peace and privacy of the home she may already share with him, in come the ravening hordes (or so it seems), hell-bent on wrecking everything from the new carpet to their dad's relationship with his girlfriend. To anyone else, not facing such a prospect, a weekend is hardly a long time; but to you, the woman who is, and whose house is suddenly invaded by odd characters she hardly knows, it's forever!

Why am I taking the line that women in this situation don't look forward to their 'family' weekends? Because I am a realist and one with a thorough grounding in this most awkward of processes. There is nothing wrong in owning up to one's misgivings about the children's next visit. Better to sort out your basic feelings on the subject than hide them behind an unselfish-sounding excuse, such as 'I prefer John to spend all his time with the children when they come. It's only fair'. Though such a statement could be quite genuine it is more likely to be a cover-up for your hope that Dad *will* take over the kids, preferably without any assistance from his girlfriend.

However, a 'weekend' stepmother can get into hot water if she voices her misgivings: I don't blame anyone who comes to the conclusion that it's impossible to do the right thing! Try all you can, making the kids as welcome and as comfortable as possible – and you're overdoing it, usurping their real mum's function. Own up to the very real doubts you may have about being able to strike up a relationship with them – and you're being cold and heartless to the children. I admire the honesty of one such stepmother, whose story is told below.

Michelle was married to a man with two young sons. They lived with their mother and stepfather, but, as their father also lived locally, paid them frequent visits. The free-and-easy way in which the children wandered into her home began to upset Michelle. She did not dislike them, but she had a busy life of her own and, childless at the time, was unable to adapt easily to their demands. After a long period of feeling bad about it and coping less and less well with these visits, she owned up. Her partner and the boys' mother were then better able to organize the visits so that Michelle was made to feel more comfortable about them. As a result, the relationships became better all round.

It may be easier said than done to talk honestly to your partner about his children's visits. Yet anything is worth the effort if it puts an end to silent, festering weekends, sulking and then guilt (yours because you are unable to feel welcoming, and his because he's trying to please everyone) and constant unhappiness which will ultimately affect everyone.

Have you ever thought how much damage such a situation could cause in terms of time alone? Imagine that Thursday and Friday are spent in a state of increasing anxiety because of nerves before the children's arrival. Then come Saturday and Sunday in a blur of chaos, with you trying to make the best of it (but without having talked it over, which means that whatever suggestions you may have can hardly be taken up) and him being desperately jolly to lighten the atmosphere. Monday is rather silent, with you still getting over the weekend and him not knowing which way to jump. You, for example, could be filled with resentment at the extra domestic chores and inevitable pile of washing, while his assertion of parental rights in a very defensive 'Why shouldn't they come here, if they want to see me?' could earn him a short, sharp answer or lead you both into a flaming row. Tuesday and Wednesday might be rather better – but we're soon back to Thursday, with the whole cycle starting again. Is it worth it? In a word, no. But the children's visits are an integral part of your lives. The problem will not disappear if ignored, and calls for compromise for *both* of you. It might be worth talking over the following points (or any other that come to mind) with your partner, in plenty of time for the next family weekend:

* What does your partner *do* when the children come? Is there, by omission, no real plan, so that the children tend to be underfoot all the time, with everyone staying claustrophobically indoors (and on one another's nerves)? Perhaps the children's grandparents live near by, or there are other possibilities. It is worth considering some activity, such as a visit or outing, which will lend a certain amount of balance to the weekend so that everyone concerned is prevented from spending all their time virtually in the same room.

* How about inviting a friend of your own? Your partner is entertaining his family, so why not ask along someone *you* can talk to? A trustworthy friend can occasionally bridge a gap, chatting with the children and helping to dilute some of the effects of your nervousness.

- Is there anything interesting *you and the children* can do together? Hostility and nerves soon evaporate when you're all falling over at the ice rink or all seeing a play or film you enjoy.

- Looking beyond the weekend, is it possible to arrange a more or less regular evening where in return for your making over some of your spare time to your partner's family you enjoy an evening together going out for a drink, meeting friends or just having a quiet meal?

It is important to break the stranglehold of children-plus-you-plus-parent trying too hard. As a dad, your partner may seem a rather odd character compared with the man you thought you knew. He may start clowning around, or remain ominously silent. In his frenzied attemps to ensure that everyone has a good time he is probably trying to over-compensate to his offspring, not to mention feeling he has to act the part of piggy-in-the-middle easing communication between you and them. What he may lose sight of is the fact that his efforts are achieving quite the opposite result. You and the children may well learn a great deal more about one another and make faster progress if you are allowed to be on your own with them. This does not have to happen in an artificial or contrived way, with your partner on guard duty every waking moment from when they arrive to when they go home.

Now for some of the more practical aspects of entertaining your weekend family. I mention these not because the readers of this book need advice on planning 48-hour hospitality, but because certain practical aspects of this particular situation can be used as row-creators or excuses, for instance: 'I'm not having your children coming here. How do you expect me to clean up after them from the minute they arrive?' or 'I'm not standing over a hot stove from Friday night for the whole weekend!' As excuses these don't hold water, I'm afraid. Try looking at things in a different light, imagining that the weekend guests are not your partner's offspring but friends of your own. Much the same sort of effort is required: preparing spare bedrooms, cooking extra food and so on. Is it really all such a chore?

Try the following line of thought the next time the children are due to stay with you (in addition to having a talk to your partner, however embarrassing you may find this).

- Meals can be a hit-and-miss affair with adults as well as children, so don't work yourself into a frenzy of gastronomic one-upmanship. A couple of evenings with an extra half-hour spent on food preparation will provide an ample basis for future meals, freeing you from the need to spend all weekend in the kitchen.

- Even simple things like making sure you have clean bed linen and towels a few days in advance will help take the heat out of the situation. Your spare bed(s) can then be made up without resorting to a hasty search in the drawers or airing cupboards (just as they walk in) or, even worse, a hastily loaded washing machine. Every guest likes to feel the host has thought about him or her, and children are no exception.

- The children might feel more comfortable and more included in things if they join in the washing-up, cooking and so forth. If you can achieve a balance between their being strictly guests and slave labour, it will do much to make them feel at home.

Having stated the positive aspect of planning, which helps to remove some of the chaos of weekend visits, a word of warning is due: do not be tempted to indulge in one-upmanship of any kind. The current adversarial divorce system has effects which linger on, and you will not be doing anyone a favour if you are bent on proving that the children's weekend environment is superior to their usual one. It is often bemoaned that the existence of 'separate camps' encourages this attitude: Mother provides everyday care which is not to be undermined by Father, who feels compelled to supplement his intermittent visits with expensive toys and gifts. Extend this line of thinking to the weekend situation, and it is not hard to see your partner encouraging you to 'spoil them a bit'. In theory, you are to indulge their every food whim, tuck them up in a Disneyland bedroom and make the whole time magical. Great – until the fairy-tale is over and the extemely confused children return to plain, ordinary Mother in her plain, ordinary home.

Whatever the politics are, try to put yourself in Mother's place: how would *you* feel if your children, after all sorts of treats with Dad, came home quarrelling and dissatisfied with what you had to offer? If it was not merely a case of one-upmanship, with your ex-husband flaunting what he can do for forty-eight hours (which you do continuously, all year round) but a campaign to ensure that the children were cleaning their teeth properly and having three square meals a day and so on, you'd be hopping mad. The children's father will very likely try his utmost to make up for the fact that he no longer sees them all the time. This is quite natural, and can be controlled. But deliberate showing off, with a broad hint that Mother's care isn't satisfactory, is non-productive from everyone's point of view.

Over to you?

Now we consider the woman who for one reason or another is expected to share her life with a partner and his children as a permanent, full-time proposition. Not easy – but possible. In an ideal world there would be no need to write any of this, no need even to discuss who might do what in the home. But we're not living in an ideal world, and many women taking on a partner's family are in for the surprise of their lives: they are created head cook and bottle-washer immediately!

While attitudes have changed greatly in a few short years, with men and women sharing more aspects of their lives both at home and at work, there are families where the women (and girls) still shoulder the greater part of the domestic burden. If as a previously single, childless woman you land in a family devoid of 'demarcation lines', you are fortunate: you will probably slot in somewhere, knowing the rest of the family do not assume that just because you're Dad's wife you'll do the donkey-work. But families, like so many other things, are often the result of conditioning. A bereaved or divorced man may make terrific progress – yet his family might not keep up with him. Suppose that during the marriage the children's mother did not go out to work: very different from today, when virtually every second wife has to earn in order to help keep the family, or to help with a husband's maintenance payments to his ex-wife and children. Suppose that your husband, while coping on his own, had been able to pay a housekeeper. This isn't so fanciful as one might imagine. In the words of one stepfather:

> I suppose you could say that Judith and I married at just the right time. My housekeeper had given notice and was leaving.

Some men were not brought up to participate in domestic chores – as some of us discover upon entering the state of matrimony! They may even have been actively discouraged from doing so. What if a man has found the whole business of caring for his family and their home more traumatic than anything he has ever experienced, and wants above all to slip back to domestic comfort?

There is no denying that such a sexist division of labour still persists in some households, and it can cause a tremendous amount of problems. If your man hasn't been reconditioned by the age we live in, then you'll have to reform him. The minute examination of domestic matters is too time-consuming a topic to pursue here; if you need practical guidance, refer to one of the myriad excellent books already on the market. Yet while we all acknowledge that our daily domestic lives, once under the microscope, show up as a tangle of rather petty concerns, it must be admitted that stepfamily life is made up of little things. The way people live, care for their homes, what they eat and so on are all matters charged with emotional energy which can so easily be misdirected. Are you going to be the intruder who upsets everyone because you don't do things in a specific, time-honoured way?

Instructions

'Tomorrow I am going to tell the children to make sure they put their dirty laundry in the basket/not to come straight into the lounge in their wellingtons/to tell me if they're running short of underwear/not to leave it until five minutes before school to mention that they've lost their games kit . . .' It's all very easy as you lie in bed composing the lines, but when the moment comes for you to deliver these simple instructions, what happens? You may be very surprised to find that as a mature, intelligent person (perhaps equipped with a degree or an outstanding ability to unblock drains) you just stand there feeling slightly sick and with sweaty palms.

Why *you*? Can't their father remind them of some of the simple things which make life so much easier? Perhaps he could. But it's important that *you* get the message across to the children, however apprehensive you may feel at first. It's well worth talking about this with your partner (a) to explain your understandable nerves and (b) to enlist his support. Having agreed more or less what the day-to-day plan will be, you must pitch in: tell the family tactfully what needs doing as and when it arises. Pick their brains, especially if they are a pretty co-operative group, and praise anything you find particularly clever. If older children have already assumed certain domestic responsibilities, be thankful for this and don't deprive them of their jobs. The tenor of your instuctions and routine will vary according to the personalities involved, as will the relative importance of order in your home, but there is one golden rule: avoid at all cost giving instructions at second hand. Children are extraordinarily perceptive and will guess within a millisecond if it's just Dad doing the bidding of his new wife and uncharacteristically dishing out orders for the day, so this one could be up to you. Hopefully, with the support of your partner, and the courage of your own convictions, you will get the message across. Perhaps the plan won't work every time at first – the children could be slightly resentful, reminding you that you're not their mother (implication: why should we do this?) – but with persistence it should succeed. The importance of your partner's moral support here cannot be emphasized too strongly.

Or, in the words of Ruth, a young stepmother faced at short notice with the prospect of a teenage stepdaughter joining the family for an indefinite period:

31

I don't ask for much. But I have the impression that just because I arrive home from work before my husband, he thinks I've been there all day! Sarah [aged about 14] is well capable of lending a hand – just things like washing-up after supper, or hanging some washing out at the weekend. But no matter what I ask her to do my husband says immediately, 'Oh, can't *you* do that? Sarah's got her homework'. That's quite true. But I've got work to do in the evening and at weekends. Needless to say, this means that I haven't got a chance if I ask her to help. She knows that she doesn't have to lift a finger!

Ruth is by no means bludgeoning her stepdaughter into being a galleyslave, just trying to encourage her to help a little so that (a) she herself is able to tackle her evening's work sooner rather than later and (b) Sarah will come to understand that small common courtesies make life a lot pleasanter for everyone. Knowing something of this particular family's background, I can guess what makes Dad react as he does. In his previous marriage there was no question of the family pitching in: Mother did not work outside the home and did virtually everything inside it. Also, he is being over-protective, guarding against a confrontation between daughter and his new wife. He does not realize that if he supported his new wife there might not even be a nasty scene: after a short sulk or a few objections, the teenager might give the small amount of help requested.

How much attention your home receives – or how little – will depend on your own preferences and the family's habits. A meticulous housekeeper walking into a place that is cheerfully chaotic won't feel quite at ease; but then neither will the free-thinker who has her first whiff of what seems a rather antiseptic environment. There has to be compromise. Are all your priorities broadly similar? Is everyone willing to contribute towards having a neat and tidy home, with all the effort this entails; or do they place more value on having time to talk, to sit and enjoy a leisurely meal or watch a favourite TV programme? If preferences match, all well and good. If, however, there's a neat-and-tidy faction pitched against a more easy-going style, there will have to be a middle ground – and everyone has to work towards finding it.

Food and mealtimes

What a strange thing to single out, I hear you say. After all, we all eat: we need to eat, and some of us love to eat. Food is a very emotional subject. Rigid food habits are soon formed and are adhered to with tenacity so that children, even relatively grown-up ones, can harbour very rigid preferences about what they will and won't try.

When I met the family who are now my stepchildren, I was a little daunted: five individuals ranging in age from childhood to young adulthood is rather a lot to take on. I didn't know if anything I did would work, but I was willing to try all the same. I shall never forget the day I cooked a main meal for the assembled party, including Father and me of course, at a weekend. Although I was not a very experienced cook, I managed to produce what I thought was a reasonable meal and served it up carefully on the dining-table with serving dishes and silver. (It is revealing to note that while this causes me little trouble now it meant an enormous amount of effort at the time!)

I don't know which was worse: the po-faced children or their father, as he waxed lyrical in his efforts to persuade them to eat the meal I had sweated over. 'Ugh, I hate that!' or 'What's *this*?' (accompanied by an expression of revulsion and a disdainful finger pointed at an innocent dish of potatoes), 'We never have those!' and so forth. The youngest, so far fairly quiet, saved his energy for one final, damning comment: 'Why can't we have *real* stuffing?' My guilty secret was out: I had made the supreme error of stuffing the chicken with an old-fashioned mixture always used in my own family, and not with a certain popular (and time-saving) packet variety. The children, so they said, felt sick. My partner felt guilty – and I felt like several large gins!

Confusion, bewilderment, resentment, fear of the unknown – all these things prompt children to reject the food a stepmother prepares for them. They could equally decide to reject something their father makes – if only to show that they are having

33

none of the new regime, whether part-time or permanent. Without becoming a doormat, it's not a bad idea to find out in advance the kind of things that do go down well: for example, if the family doesn't go in for silver service then don't impose this unfamiliar and formal style on them. If, however, they like their meals served with finesse, don't throw them by just slinging something on a tray in front of the television. You will be able to introduce the things you like as you go along. The family will probably surprise you with their favourites; let them prepare a meal for you and see what happens. (You can always save a particular favourite of your own for a rare occasion when you and your partner have a chance to eat alone.) After a while, it will be hard to remember who introduced whom and to what. My own culinary repertoire has increased considerably as a result of trying out my own and the family's ideas. And I can't remember with absolute clarity now who had the bright idea of adding this or that, or who first thought of scrapping Sunday lunch . . .

A meal with a new adult – you – crystallizes the whole stepfamily situation. From the children's point of view, everything is strange and possibly frightening. They will come to appreciate you and your efforts, but in the meantime remember that to them it must seem that they suddenly have to cope with (a) a new adult, (b) unfamiliar food and possibly (c) a new and strange way of having a meal – not a combination tipped for instant success.

Angels' footsteps

Settling into a bereaved family brings its own problems. Some of the difficulties experienced by women who marry divorced men may not apply, but it can be hard to assume a place in the family which has lost a wife/mother. One young woman told me:

> During the first year of our marriage there was only one room in the house where I truly felt at home: our bedroom. It was as if the rest of it still belonged to Nicola.

This woman was up against a pervasive problem: her husband

and stepfamily had chosen to remain in the house where they had always lived. As the newcomer, she felt she could hardly insist that they moved. There are often practical as well as emotional reasons for staying put. Still, the couple – and the family – have a better chance of making a go of Father's second (or subsequent) marriage if a new home can be found.

> I am sure people mean no harm, but it irritates me beyond belief to hear about one's dead predecessor: 'Oh, she was a wonderful woman! You would have loved her!'

The provider of this quotation (a mother and stepmother in her forties) may well have loved her husband's other wife, had they ever met; it is the universal agreement that her predecessor was perfect which she finds so irritating. Of course no one wishes to speak ill of someone who has died – it's in bad taste, irreverent. Yet it is extremely difficult when your rival is not flesh and blood, a living human being with good qualities and defects alike. When your rival is legend, what do you do? How do you settle into your new home when you sense uneasily that someone is about to remind you that this or that ornament was 'her' favourite, that 'she' never wore that particular colour or used those glasses, or of another such domestic detail? (Those of us whose problems arise from someone still very much alive might on a bad day wish fervently that we only had a ghost to contend with!) You can't phone up your dead predecessor when you're at the end of your tether. This is a cue for your partner's family and friends to be especially thoughtful. It's a new start – for everyone.

The 'Ex'

When you take on a man with children, you take on a past. This past has a physical form, in the shape of children, and also its practical aspect in the form of the dealings which may still crop up between the formerly married couple. Particularly if you are a weekend stepmother, you are likely to know about your predecessor. There can be awkward situations and embarrassment not to mention frayed tempers and outright anger if the two women, one 'ex' and one current spouse, clash.

First of all, it is worth fixing firmly in your mind that whatever the former wife is like – glamorous, intellectual, a wonderful housewife or whatever – she is not relevant to your current relationship. That represents a new start, and unless there is a very peculiar regime in force, with her on the doorstep every five minutes, what she is like in terms of looks or personality matters little.

The influence she may exert over the children, however, is quite another matter. Although, strictly speaking, it is against the rules to put a spanner in the works when a husband remarries, it does happen. There are occasions when an ex-wife, reacting to her new situation, starts behaving with, to put it mildly, all the tact and subtlety of a child, controlling neither her tongue or her temper. The basest of motivations make her want to spoil things for her ex-husband, even if she really doesn't want or need him any more. In cases where both former partners seem to have found some sort of balance and lead reasonably happy lives, this type of situation may not be so prevalent; yet while it lasts it can be upsetting.

Some of the most harrowing cases of this can occur where children are primed by their mother (or even by another relative) to ask awkward questions or behave badly during their visits. Resorting to the use of a child to secure information about money (one of the commonest topics of dissension) is disgraceful, but it certainly happens. It is of course difficult in the extreme if after a divorce the questions of support and maintenance are not settled satisfactorily. But what can be the possible advantage of getting a child to pipe up at a strategic moment, 'Mummy wonders why we aren't getting any money'? Or what good will it do if on visits to Dad the child is instructed to take careful note of anything new or lavish spotted in the home Dad now shares with his current wife? At best it will lead to an unhappy atmosphere. (In the real-life case of a child told to do this, it meant the end of her regular visits to her father, so upset was she by the whole business.) At worst it will lead to rows and slow-burning resentment all round, not least on the part of the 'new' wife, who often sees a chunk of her own earnings disappear to support her predecessor and family.

After your partner's divorce, it is worth talking over with him the basic questions of money and arrangements so that whatever form the lobbying may take you will be in for no surprises. Couples can be strangely reticent on this subject: it isn't always an easy topic to discuss, hence the temptation to draw a veil over the less attractive details. Should nasty incidents crop up, don't react more than you absolutely have to. Try to bear in mind that it is highly likely that whoever is behind the campaign (the ex-wife or even possibly the grandparents) would probably do the same irrespective of your husband's choice of partner. Then try to talk over the difficulties with your partner as objectively as you can.

As second (or subsequent) wives and stepmothers, it would be ideal if we could get across to our predecessors a message somewhere along these lines: 'Please believe that just because I married your former husband I am in no way crowing over my current situation, gloating because you no longer have a husband or hell-bent on making anyone's life a misery. Your children are important in all our lives, and I am willing to do whatever is required to help them. They, more than anyone, need protection because while adults do eventually 'bounce back' from the trauma of divorce children do not, in my opinion. Please let us act together to prevent any further disruption in their lives.'

Conclusion

A woman's place is not invariably in the home. You may have your own job and your own friends, and it is vital not to discard these, whatever the demands of your new family life may be. It is too easy to assume that a stepfamily, particularly if it is a full-time one, calls for a clearly defined arrangement with one partner working and the other not, one leading a reasonable social life and the other not, and so forth – but this does not have to be the case.

Pool your resources, not forgetting to include the children's contribution as they grow up, and you will have flexibility. Flexibility breeds willingness: a great asset in a stepfamily. If you mark the dividing line between your partner and yourself, thus effectively halving resources, there will not be sufficient flexibility or willingness to go round in this new 'hybrid' family.

5

Mainly For Men

Like stepmothers, stepfathers bemoan their bad press. Using sensational and distasteful banner headlines which attract the worst kind of curiosity, Fleet Street seems to take a strange relish in printing, loud and clear: 'STEPFATHER IN CHILD CRUELTY CASE.' That any child should be the subject of cruelty is bad enough, and is rightly condemned wholesale. Yet how many members of the public put down their newspapers having absorbed the fact that a *stepfather* is capable of such things with a cynical 'Well, what can you expect?'

A stepfather may know little about the children he will soon have under his wing, or he may know them intimately. He may approach the new family with ease and confidence or with apprehension, but whatever the case he should not be typecast as the villain of the piece. A great deal of added responsibility faces a man as he prepares to take on his partner's children: it isn't at all like a 'normal' partnership or marriage, where two adults spend their time adapting to each other. Stepfamilies vary considerably in character and circumstances; indeed, there are practically as many kinds of stepfamily as there are of situations which created them. As a result, it is impossible to set down ideas, suggestions or guidelines that hold the key for every stepfather. Yet it may be useful to glance at a few case histories:

The previously single stepfather

Here we look at Michael, a mature man who was single and childless before he married Rosemary, a divorcée with one teenage daughter. Their relationship was no whirlwind romance but a slow, deliberate affair which allowed the couple plenty of time to think things over. The stepdaughter was approaching a difficult time in her life, the transition from childhood to young womanhood which causes enough difficulties for 'real' fathers, let alone stepfathers with little practical grounding in such matters. After much deliberation, the couple married. They had received advice – some in favour, much against – but decided to take their chances. From talking to Michael, a few points of interest emerged:

- Prepare as much as you can in advance for your future life with a wife and child. We attended a special group near by, but sadly there were too few participants to make it viable. But I suppose we must have gone there regularly for about a year before we married.

- *Talk* about problems (financial matters, the family's preferences, any irritating habits, child discipline and so on). It does no good to hope that these will somehow get sorted out on their own!

- I was very concerned indeed about our marriage not only being right for us [self and wife] but also for Diane [Rosemary's teenage daughter]. I was prepared to do everything I could. I feel now, after a 'settling-in' period, that whatever problems Diane and I have are broadly similar to the usual father/daughter issues which crop up in so-called normal families.

Was Michael tempted to accept his wife and to try to reject her daughter?

No. I knew from the start that to marry Rosemary I had to prepare for her and Diane. There was no question of anything else.

What does he think of men who are rather casual about the future, adopting the attitude of hoping it'll work but not being concerned over the children if it doesn't?

You can't expect it to work. Unfortunately, I think that quite a few men tend to think like this. I know some who do, and I'm sure that Rosemary could quote chapter and verse on men who are interested until they realize that there's a child (or children) to be considered. As soon as it's clear that she's responsible for a child who will be included in the relationship, they take off!

Although Michael has experienced the settling-in process of stepfamily life, he has not had to deal with one very common problem: in his case, the situation has been devoid of father-figures. His own father died when Michael was only a child. What is more, his wife's ex-husband did not feature prominently in her life following the divorce, so that consequently his stepdaughter grew up somewhat as Michael did – with no father-figure in the picture. He may have had to contend with several female figures (mother/grandmother/wife/stepdaughter), but at no time has he had to cope with tension, competition or confrontation between himself and an ex-husband/father. In view of the fact that Rosemary and Diane as mother and daughter must have been close and rather self-sufficient, was any difficulty created by Michael's becoming the male (husband/father) figure in their lives?

Perhaps. I think that Diane must find it hard because *I* object to certain things and, like most fathers of teenage girls, feel obliged to say no.

Interestingly, the issues Michael had to contend with were usually Diane's school work, her friends, her wanting to go out: very much the behaviour and discipline aspect of life as opposed to the more intimate food/clothing/domestic scene, which tends to fall to the lot of the *stepmother*.

It is clear from talking to Michael that his type of thoughtful, caring approach has done much to secure the good working relationship that he now has with his stepdaughter. He admitted that the early stages had been far from easy: for example, Diane was caught off-balance on the subject of her mother's re-marriage, even though she knew quite well that Rosemary and Michael intended to get married one day. I was privileged to talk to Diane, something both she and Michael admit would not have been possible even a year previously. Of the marriage and her acquisition of a stepfather, she says:

I know I wasn't genuine when I said I was pleased about it. But by the time they got married I was really pleased. I wasn't just saying it.

Michael joins in the activities which 'ordinary' mums and dads share: for instance, he accompanies Rosemary on visits to Diane's school when her work is to be discussed. He does not feel that as a stepfather he is in any way required to stand aside. Wherever possible, things are talked over between the three of them.

The previously married stepfather

Here we consider a situation where a divorced, childless man becomes a stepfather and the couple then adds to the family by having one or more children of their own.

David is a young man who now lives in a house where children could be said to predominate! He had left a childless marriage and acquired two stepchildren, both boys, before he and his new wife had children of their own, a son and a daughter. David's key advantage is that at the time of his remarriage the boys were very young; we are talking about toddlers rather than older children or teenagers. All the family seem very happy and relaxed together, though they have survived certain common problems such as striving to achieve a balance with the boys' real dad and enduring the aftermath of the divorces that were necessary before the couple could get together. David is optimistic about the future of his family, children and stepchildren alike; but he is ruthlessly honest about himself. Asked about his approach to the stepfamily, he said:

It was up to me to make it work. You make mistakes, but if things go wrong, don't be too quick to blame everyone else except yourself. When there's a problem or something which causes unhappiness, I look at *my* role in it. If, basically, I am not tolerant enough/thoughtless/insensitive, then that problem must have something to do with me. If I accept that, then I can do something about it!

David is anxious to state, as was Michael, that it is impossible to separate parent and children in one's approach to the new partnership. Would he have liked to marry his wife without taking on her two boys? 'Suppose she sensed this, wanted you badly enough and hastily shed the children in order to get you?' He replied that he would be very uneasy about entering into any commitment at all with that person. In other words, while he was apprehensive about his future as a stepfather, he saw it as a real commitment to be made, matching the mother's commitment. This applies in more than one direction. In general discussion, both stepfathers and stepmothers asserted that even though their partnerships had proved difficult at times they would have felt uneasy about accepting a partner who seemed willing to offload his/her family elsewhere.

Didn't David, as a relatively young man whose previous marriage had not been altogether unhappy, think he was letting himself in for an unnecessary burden in taking on two 'instant' children?

In some ways, yes! I had the ingredients for a happy life. Good job, good relationship with my ex-wife [the couple were still married when David and his new wife met] and what some people call 'no ties'. But I did want a family. I knew all along that the children were not mine although I welcomed the chance of being 'in' on a young family.

In fact, David's desire for a family was very much confirmed by his experiences with the two little boys. He stresses the benefits of adding to the family so that everyone feels comfortable together.

The two boys, although they're still quite young, possibly feel as if there's more security. It's as if they know that we plan to stay together a long time because of our two youngest children. Besides, we all have a 'share' in them: I, my wife and the two older boys.

Young though the stepsons still may be, what difficulties, if any, have arisen between them and David?

I didn't expect the kind of difficulties which arise with teenage children, but I must say how much harder I have had to work with my wife's older son. There has always been that bit of distance there – not exactly a barrier, but the knowledge that I'm not his dad.

Given that in this situation the boys' father is very much in the picture, what is it like for David? Is he ever tempted to 'take over'?

Basically, no. If I am disgruntled with anything that happens, I try, as far as anyone can, to put myself in *his* shoes. How would I like it if someone muscled in on me and *my* children?

What about money? Is it hard to feel that you're providing for all the children, even though two of them have a dad near by who, in theory, *could* provide?

I have never felt a strain. I don't remind myself that my earnings support four children, two of whom aren't mine! The only problems I foresee – something which we are all going to have to think about – are big questions, such as education. Whatever the two older boys receive the rest of the family will have to have the same. As we are not ruling out private schools I might be disappointed if, for example, the father of my two stepsons refused either to entertain the idea or to come to an arrangement about providing fees.

In this particular family the older children are the subject of a joint custody order. David's wife and her ex-husband live within reach of each other, making it possible for them to meet at almost any time and discuss the children. David sees the importance of this and agrees with his wife that *both* parents should always take decisions together wherever possible. Surely this is fine in an ideal world – but don't such arrangements cause problems from time to time?

Yes! If there can be such a thing, I feel that we have been too

43

'civilized' – the classic, textbook, earnest attempt at being fairer than fair, super-polite and extremely careful not to tread on each other's toes. As the outsider, stepfather and husband, not father, I occasionally felt as if I was working overtime to meet the boys' father's needs. Always being terribly obliging. I couldn't continue doing this indefinitely. I needed to preserve my self-respect and to feel that my efforts should at least be acknowledged from time to time.

Strangely enough, a parallel situation exists elsewhere in the family. The boys' father, now remarried, found at one point that his wife was feeling a little like David did: she too had begun to suffer the effects of everyone being so obliging.

On the surface, everything appears easy and pleasant in David's composite family – though he and his wife assure me that this is not always so. They stress the need, which they feel some couples ignore, for partners to talk to each other rather than let sources of discomfort and resentment develop to the point where a serious row may occur. It is clear that, like many stepfathers, David puts a great deal of thought into his care of the stepchildren. In his opinion a stepfamily relationship will not prosper unless the stepfather makes an extra effort.

The stepfather and parent

What is it like for the man who is already a father to become a step-parent? Although this topic recurs later in the book (see Chapter 7, where I discuss the joining of families) it is useful to extract the father/stepfather's viewpoint for consideration here.

Kenneth has coped with his own family, two very young girls, since being widowed, and then got married to a woman with two children, a boy and a girl. The age distribution was such that the two middle children, one of Kenneth's daughters and his wife's son, were very close to each other in age.

I suppose the most striking thing is that while you can tolerate virtually anything which your own children do, it is extremely hard to put up with your partner's children! Yours can make a

44

noise and you don't flinch. But when my wife's children made even moderate noise, I began to get annoyed.

This statement was borne out by Kenneth's wife sagely nodding her head and smiling. Neither of the adults had any clues as to *why* this should be the case; they just offered advice to others that extra tolerance and patience are required.

What about day-to-day family life? What does Kenneth have to bear in mind?

You may be super-tolerant with your own children, but it is easy to be a bit too protective. For example, I recognized when my own children needed to be told off but did not, at first, like the thought of my wife doing it. On every necessary occasion I found myself dealing with my *own* children, just as my wife dealt with *hers*. This continued for quite some time, with both of us knowing very well that it was going on but reluctant to talk about it. There was a bit of an atmosphere . . . In the end we did discuss it so that it would stop. I don't know why parents feel the need to 'protect' their children from a step-parent.

While the eldest and youngest children of the family settled quite well into this new composite group it was clear that the two 'middle' ones did not fare so well. What was wrong?

There was terrific rivalry. I think it was much more pronounced than if they had been natural brother and sister. It led to arguments, sulking, silences, and made us unhappy. It is very difficult to combat.

There is a happier postscript to this, however. Both of them, now teenagers, are currently under pressure because of exams, and are now being told by *both* adults to work hard, stay in, make sure they pass – all the things two natural parents would doubtless tell them to do. As a result they have joined forces, and while the outward signs of rivalry and conflict remain visible Kenneth and his wife feel that in private the two of them are friendlier and more co-operative than they have ever been, something which is fostered by the fact that they have quite a large group of friends in common. (Perhaps these youngsters have discovered and learned to manipulate the notorious principle of 'divide and rule'?)

Apart from emotional issues and the problem of imposing discipline where two groups of children are concerned, what about the question of money? These stepchildren do not have a father on the doorstep and constantly in evidence, yet there is one sphere of influence in which he is active, and this Kenneth can find hard to bear gracefully:

Whenever I try to get the message across [to *all* the children] about saving for things they want – waiting until Christmas and seeing if we [the adults] can chip in and help them out – along comes the much-wanted stereo/speakers/large sum of money or promise of expenditure far in excess of what we can manage. How can I encourage them [in particular the step-children] to be self-reliant and responsible with money in these circumstances?

What about the much-vaunted myth that as a step-parent you have to love your stepchildren?

Impossible! They will always be somebody else's children, however close you become. People should not feel guilty about it, if they do not love, or even like, their stepchildren quickly. Guilt only makes it worse.

What is it like, at first, to have two groups of children under your joint care?

You soon realize that there are probably two entirely different methods of bringing up children involved. It is unlikely that your new partner will employ the same ideas as you do. The differences appear instantly and can be hard to live with, making one partner inevitably seem rather a hard-liner. In my case, I think that my own children had been let off lightly. I had employed someone to help during the time I was alone with the children, and they therefore had no permanent mother-figure. When I remarried, their stepmother appeared to them to be much tougher than anyone else had been, and that was difficult. But I am not blameless. I recall one dreadful incident with the children and myself [alone] on holiday. We were on the beach, and when my own daughter screamed I rashly assumed that it was my stepson who had hurt her. I was too quick off the mark, thought it was more serious than it was – and smacked him. That was terrible!

Kenneth and his wife agreed that in a stepfamily such as theirs certain faily basic characteristics tend to emerge both among the adults and the children. One of these is rivalry, based on jealousy. Adults are no less immune than children from jealousy, as they are quick to point out: the very fact that your partner has children is proof positive of his/her previous sex life, and you might not want reminders of that all the time. Your new partner can't spare all the time in the world to be your husband/wife or a sympathetic extra parent to your children. He/she has other responsibilities: those 'other' children under your roof.

Stepfather and 'part-time' parent

Given that after a marital breakdown the children involved usually remain with their mother, what happens when a man considers remarrying or actually does remarry? He presumably lives with his wife's children, and may provide for them. So how does he reconcile this with the fact that his own children are not always part of the family?

Richard is a middle-aged man who underwent a very bitter divorce, the main enmity arising from the matter of custody, which he was quite unable to obtain. He resigned himself to seeing his own children only when this was possible. However, at one stage he had a relationship with a divorced woman who had two children of her own. He did not find it easy to become accepted by the children, though he did strike up a good relationship with one of them. When thinking about making things more permanent, he remembers feeling:

47

that it was almost impossible. How would my own children feel about my settling down with a wife's children in the house? [There was a great deal of anguish, since the children Richard left behind were, he felt, unsettled, finding it extremely difficult to accept the fact that they couldn't see him much.] As for my potential stepchildren, I found one unexpectedly easier to get along with than the other, who proved very difficult, although my initial impressions were otherwise.

He now feels that too many difficulties were in evidence at that particular time: it was still only a short time since the breakdown of his own former marriage, and there was too much anxiety about his own family. He also feels he would have been unable to make his own children accept the fact that their father was apparently settled in a new home with 'new' children. (The difference between a father's stepchildren and his later-born natural children is, incidentally, a very marked one.)

In circumstances where the divorce has not been quite so upsetting and where the children are securely in one home or another, things are not quite as difficult: for instance, a father could remarry and take on stepchildren while continuing to see his own family, who do not wish to live with him. As long as a father's children by a previous marriage are made welcome to see him – and this means the new couple must be prepared to tolerate some spectacular displays, at least initially – then some sort of balance can be achieved. Of course, the 'mine' and 'not mine' principle is bound to exert an influence. A father may feel indulgent towards his own offspring who at weekends or in the school holidays bring with them their own particular brand of chaos, while his new wife may on occasion pull him up sharply for apparently being too hard on *her* children. What is more, she may find his kids, who seem to upset everyone on their visits, positively infuriating. The received wisdom here is to carry on – however uncomfortable this may prove. As long as both adults are prepared to be tolerant and honest with each other and do not allow sources of argument to fester, it is essential that all the children concerned should be given a fair chance.

The remarried father

What about the dad who lives apart from his kids and then gets married again, this time to a woman without children? On the face of it, the outlook here appears less complicated. Does the fact of his remarriage make it easier or more difficult for him to see the children, who live with their mother? Is he going to have difficulty in persuading his new, childless wife to help him out when the occasion arises?

Paul is a divorcee in his forties with two daughters who are now almost grown up. He met and married Anna, a capable and charming woman several years his junior. He had met Anna while he was separated from his wife. Their relationship developed, via a period of living together, into marriage, by which time the couple had known each other four or five years. Paul's two daughters were teenagers when their father re-married, and continued to live with their mother, visiting Paul and Anna regularly. As a couple they were prepared to do everything possible to make his children welcome. Anna in particular was most conscientious about her stepdaughters' visits, realizing how difficult at times it was for them to have a 'normal' relationship with their father; and even though privately she had misgivings about 'bending over backwards', she took care not to upset either her husband or the girls.

While the basic principle of the two girls seeing their father whenever possible was readily acceptable to Anna, the vexed question of money was not: a new, well-paid job for her resulted in Paul's ex-wife applying for more maintenance money for her daughters. Every visit the girls made was preceded by a request for Paul to supply the return train fare – otherwise they just couldn't go, and so forth. For Anna this was hard to bear, since Paul's ex-wife had herself remarried – and could surely expect her new husband to help provide for the family? Had Anna stinted with either money or hospitality in the past she would perhaps have understood why the other woman was being so demanding, but she had always welcomed the two girls whenever they came and had not hesitated to help out if she could.

Faced with his ex-wife's demands and the contributions he had to ask of Anna in terms of both time and money, Paul felt guilty all round. Anna, who had not given a great deal of thought to having children before marrying Paul, now wanted children of her own. But how could they even think of it? They couldn't afford to make the improvements they wanted to their home, let alone envisage Anna giving up work to have a baby. Another crisis broke when, a few years after Paul and Anna's wedding, one of the girls was sent to live with her dad. The elder sister had already left home and was working away, and on the evidence available it appeared that the younger one was making life difficult for Mum and her new husband.

There seemed to be no chance of persuading Paul's ex-wife to persist in her efforts to sort things out. It was more or less an ultimatum: either Paul had his younger daughter to live with him or her own marriage would fail. Paul did his best to make the transition as easy as possible for the daughter in question – after all, it wasn't her fault, was it? Being a teenager she was not easy to handle, so he determined to do his best – he had little choice, after all. Anna took it all remarkably well and resolved, with Paul, to make her stepdaughter welcome. She felt rather sorry for this girl who had been dubbed a troublemaker.

Whatever Paul may have managed in theory he failed to achieve in practice. When his daughter finally arrived to live with him, he at times found it very hard to know which way to jump: should he support Anna in her handling of situations or side with his daughter? The whole affair of a likely confrontation between the two of them upset him deeply, and rather than acknowledge this, meeting problems as they arose and thus actively working out some of them, he opted out. He preferred to forget that difficulties could exist between his wife and daughter, hoping – quite understandably – that somehow they would all disappear. As his daughter had had a difficult time with his ex-wife, becoming the subject of rows and allegedly threatening to break up her new marriage, he did not wish a similar situation to reoccur. He wanted her new start under his roof to be just that. As a result he felt that appearing to act 'normally', administering all the usual tellings-off where necessary, requesting his daughter's active co-operation in family life and some help for her stepmother, would be wrong – surely this would all stir up trouble and upset his daughter?

Unfortunately, his policy of non-intervention did not work very well. Anna felt frustrated and helpless, sensing that whatever she asked for would never be forthcoming; it seemed that any request she made of her stepdaughter would automatically be countered by her husband. These difficulties made it more apparent to her than ever that she had to concentrate on her husband's family rather than envisage having children of her own. Paul's daughter didn't prosper, either. Because everything was intended to be so low-key, presumably to help her settle in and to spare any awkward scenes, she felt rootless: acceptance of whatever she did (or did not) do was not enough to make her feel genuinely at home, part of a 'real' family with her father and stepmother. She left home quite soon after leaving school. In theory, this left Paul and Anna back where they had started: alone as a couple and able to enjoy their relationship in privacy. Yet the intervening years had left them with an uncomfortable legacy: their separate efforts had failed, and this knowledge was not easy to live with.

What might they have done to see their daughter/stepdaughter off on an independent life and feeling more satisfied?

- It would have been worthwhile trying to avoid fights at a distance between Paul and his ex-wife. There was contact between them on several occasions, but too few useful meetings which might have taken the heat out of certain situations, particularly the most serious one when Paul was told his daughter would be coming to live with him immediately.

- Paul should have approached Anna with greater honesty. She was, after all, already quite willing to help his daughter and needed no persuading to accept her as a permanent resident. It is often impossible to prepare in advance for a child's sudden arrival in the family, but some honest discussion between Paul and Anna in the earliest days would at least have put them properly in touch with each other on the matter.

- After one or two blush-making skirmishes, possibly with frayed tempers and some hard words, Paul would have gained from laying down a few ground rules for his daughter. Whatever had happened in the past, she was now under his roof and should have been made to obey certain basic rules. Doubtless there would have been a bit of resistance, but wouldn't it have made the teenager feel that she at least belonged?

- At the risk of sounding as if it is always the woman who has my support, I feel obliged to say that Anna should have been able to do her bit *with the necessary support from Paul*. It is quite clear that on a day-to-day basis she had more to do with her stepdaughter than he did. Frank and open discussion between the partners would have led sooner or later to a scheme for *both* adults to follow.

Pointers for stepfathers

This is a list of suggestions distilled from the advice of the many families I have met who have tips to offer new stepfathers. The advice comes from *them*, not from me.

Early days

- If it is at all possible to establish some sort of rapport with the child/children's dad, do so. This makes everything a great deal easier and paves the way to discussing such matters as money, holidays, schools and, eventually, issues related to behaviour or discipline. He will feel as if he has much more control over things, and will also appreciate the fact that you, as his children's stepfather, care. It should also prevent him from feeling that another man is 'taking over'.

- Talk about what is involved and what demands are going to be made on all the adults concerned. It's essential to talk everything over frankly between husband and wife (by which I mean the stepfather and the children's mother). If you want to become actively involved with your stepchildren, then give your partner ample opportunity to tell you what she expects. Things you neither anticipated nor even thought of will then not come as a complete surprise.

- Having accepted that you're going to be a stepfather in this relationship, not merely a husband/partner, take on the role in an accepting frame of mind. Don't fall into the trap of assuming everything will work without your co-operation. If you don't really want an 'instant' family on either a full or a part-time basis, then don't marry this woman who already has children. You can't possibly have a good relationship with just part of the family: it is a complete package deal and must be accepted as such.

- Don't expect to fall madly in love with your stepchildren. Just as they don't have to accept you without reservation, you can't expect to like or love them immediately; it takes time. Ignore all those around you who maintain that you should think of your partner's children 'just as your own'; you may not even have your own family, and if you do your stepchildren might seem quite different. Above all, don't feel guilty. You will strike up a surprisingly good relationship with them as long as you're willing. It doesn't happen overnight.

Family life

- When you have all settled down as a group (as opposed to the situation of the first few weeks or months, when everyone felt rather as if they were taking part in some sort of experiment), speak up about anything that is puzzling or bothering you. You will have had enough time to discover whether or not certain ideas work. It gets dangerous to keep things to yourself. For instance, if there's another way of doing things at weekends, or if difficulties arise over taking children to and from school, mention it. There's no use letting a small matter annoy you, because this could mushroom into a bad atmosphere or a quarrel.

- Who tells the children off? Who sends them to bed? Someone has to be the keeper of order in a family. Perhaps you have preferred your wife to do this; if so, it's time to

53

think about phasing in your contribution. It will work, as long as the children's mother *backs you up*.

- Even if you found it hard at first to break the ice with your stepchildren, don't stop trying; you will soon get to know what works and what doesn't. For instance, it's no good behaving like Father Christmas, all jokey and jolly. But resist the temptation to hang back and remain apart from your wife and children. They will welcome you – if you let them.

- If there are imperfections in the way you manage your stepchildren's visits to their father, grandparents and so on, don't hesitate to talk about them, first with your partner and eventually with the other adults concerned. There is no use resenting the long, tedious drives that may be necessary for taking children back and forth; if you can be met half-way, ensure that this happens. Conversely, if you are approached to help out when these family visits occur, accept reasonable requests – it could make things easier for everyone.

Emotional Problems

- Jealousy. This is a big feature in stepfamily life, and stepfathers are certainly not immune. Rationally, you know that your partner has children and you expect her to look after them as a mother should. Yet, irrationally, you're jealous: she doesn't have all the time in the world for you (and her time for your children could be a bit short, if you too have a family), which makes you feel left out. This very basic, very potent feeling of jealousy should evaporate as you and the family get to know one another.

- Your partner's doubts and emotional crises. Few women who have been through divorce or bereavement emerge with a complete ability to think of nothing but the future, and your partner may have enormous misgivings about the new set-up. Will her children flourish? Will you? What if she makes a mess of it? Is she being upset by her ex-husband or in-laws? She may still be affected by the memory of confusing elements from a past relationship, such as a particularly good period (during a patch which is proving difficult for *you* both!). Remember: she is a woman as well as a wife and mother. Spare some time to listen and offer reassurance.

- The children's reluctance to accept you. They are, after all, children, not mature people. They may have been through a very unhappy, bewildering phase – which takes time to complete – and so don't appear to give you a rapturous welcome. Also, they have a certain loyalty to their parents, Mum *and Dad* – and perhaps they can't quite work out where you fit in? Are they to call you 'Dad'? (Do they have to?) Does this mean that somehow they have to forget the father they've got? Things which are quite clear to adults can appear very confused to children. Yet there is light at the end of the tunnel. One stepfather told me how thrilled he was the first time his stepson came to him and kissed him goodbye before leaving for school. It was a handsome pay-off for all the mornings he, the stepfather, had done that, making the first move.

- Flak from outside the couple/children. Stepfathers can be very hurt by the opposition relatives or friends may present. (Some desperate relatives may even resort to encouraging the kids to think you're an ogre!)

- It's upsetting, and it can make you start to wonder why you ever bothered, but, speaking from first-hand experience, the best advice is to ignore it if you can. If the relationship between you, your partner and her children is a workable one, with you making all the effort you can, then you'll be able to ride out the storm. If, on the other hand, it's a case of your relatives telling you you should never have become a step-parent, then they may need several firm reminders that you have chosen this way of life freely, despite all its difficulties, and intend to carry on with it. Their encouragement would be more helpful than their misgivings.

Conclusion

I don't doubt that the situations and problems discussed in this chapter are only the tip of the proverbial iceberg. On the surface, it doesn't look an enticing prospect, entering a partnership likely to be short on privacy, perks and glamour and somewhat long on effort, patience and tolerance. But when you're starting to feel that you're making progress, receiving the first signs of warmth and acceptance from the family, then it's worth it.

6

If I Were You . . .

The heat is now off parents and partners. We come to the motives and methods of those outside the immediate couple-children situation: namely friends, relatives, advisors or anyone else who may voice an opinion on the subject. For the sake of convenience I shall refer to this entire group, regardless of the degree of involvement, as 'bystanders'.

We all love romance. We praise the girl who finally brings home a dashing, handsome (single, childless) fiancé. We applaud the dutiful son who on marrying picks his mother's ideal bride: modest, pretty, charming – and childless! But people are *people*, not characters in glossy films or pulp fiction. Does your son's delightful, attractive girlfriend suddenly become any less appealing when you discover she has two children? And is the interesting man your daughter is hoping to marry any less of a catch if he happens to be divorced, with an ex-wife and children?

Allow for the initial shock (best not displayed, if you can possibly avoid it, incidentally), then let matters rest. Accept the fact that a close relative or friend is choosing to spend his/her life with someone who has already known marriage and parenthood. If the two of them are free to associate in any way they choose, you would do far better to accept the situation than fight it. Of course it can cause anxiety, especially if the couple in question present an age gap – but how old is 'too old', and how young is 'too young'? There is no reason why a mature, articulate person of, say, twenty-three, shouldn't be able to cope with the home and family of a youthful forty-year-old. Let's face it: in a parent's eyes, 'too young' could be anywhere between eighteen and thirty-eight, while 'too old' may refer less to a person's age than to his/her family commitments.

Do you recognize any of these myths about marrying into a stepfamily?

'If my son marries her (a mother), he'll never have a family of his own.'

'If my daughter marries this man who has children, she'll just be their slave.'

'She (a mother) only wants my son as a provider for her kids.'

'Everyone knows stepchildren cause trouble.'

'My son could have married *anybody*' implication: a single, childless girl.

'Since this person's previous marriage didn't work, I don't suppose this one will either.'

Despite this talk of gloom and doom, young stepfathers *do* have children of their own, making additions to the stepfamily. It has been known for women who take on men and their children to lead quite normal lives and not be chained to the kitchen sink. And, yes, while a woman may ask a new husband to help provide for her family, she doesn't necessarily go all out for a meal ticket. *Do* stepchildren cause trouble, all by themselves, or is it the climate of doubt and suspicion (which a less than enthusiastic bystander can do much to create) which is to blame? And we all know that young, unattached men can marry *anybody* they choose; it just so happens that some of them meet young, attractive women who have been married before!

Some of the pessimism which arises stems from our natural desire to protect those we love. If you are facing the prospect of a dear friend or relative becoming a step-parent, you fear for him/her – possibly because of the bad press step-parents seem to get. But while it would be patently irresponsible to con such a person into believing life in another's family will be a bed of roses, you will not help by uttering dire warnings of misery.

Whatever your role as a bystander – whether your concern is for a parent, a potential step-parent or a child – the message is simple: clear the decks mentally as much as you possibly can. The new relationship is a clean page: a fresh start for everyone, including *you*. The road to happiness is not necessarily always via the union of one single, childless man and one single, childless woman.

Advising parents

Let us suppose a single parent you know well is now feeling optimistic about remarrying or entering into some other form of long-term partnership. How do you feel about it?

You may well be very pleased. It could have been hard for you to witness this person coping alone with a family. Perhaps you have been a provider, adviser and helper in many difficult situations – how good it is to feel the pressure will soon be off! But *is* it good? Much as you may have complained in the past about your extra responsibilities, do you really relish the thought of your friend acquiring a partner and, very possibly, excluding you from the charmed circle? You do, genuinely, want them to be happy, but you cannot help having certain reservations:

'Will they make a go of it? How do I know that the new partner is really reliable?'

'Will the children like him/her?'

'Two families may now be under one roof. What if the other children cause trouble?'

'You know what they say about second marriages, that there's not much chance of it working.'

These misgivings are for the couple and the family – and are just a little to do with you. Whether or not they manage to lay the ghosts of the past and rebuild a happy group with a successful adult partnership at its centre depends on your attitude as well as their own progress. For example, we all know how a previous (and unspeakable) husband or wife can become a saint once the divorce is over and a new partner on the horizon. (If only the departed spouse knew how once-hostile relatives or friends were rooting for him/her now!)

This attitude has to go right out of the window. Chewing it over in private or with someone close, you probably find yourself comparing the two partners, ex- and future: 'John wasn't a great husband, but he was a good father,' or 'Mary had her off-days – but that was nothing compared with *this* one!' Comforting, but totally unproductive. Nurse these comparisons, and you will articulate them; breathe one word to the would-be bride or bridegroom, that is the lone parent, and he/she might never confide in you again. What is it, exactly, about the partner that is worrying you? Is he/she childless and therefore unlikely to know how to deal with a family? Try to think of this as a positive advantage: if the person in question knows little about children, he or she will learn, hopefully from a fresh point of view. They may see potential in their 'instant' family which you never noticed, and you for your part might applaud some of their novel ways of doing things. A new partner needs your support, not your doubts.

Should this newcomer to the family ever confide in you, even perhaps, expressing some pretty frank misgivings about what he/she has taken on, it's up to you to boost that person's confidence and give encouragement, without resorting to telling all about their predecessor. If you are entrusted with a confidence, keep it; don't be tempted to share it with the other partner, complete with a graphic description of how the step-parent came to you for help.

And if the one you are close to, the once-single parent, comes to you for help after getting together with a new partner, don't sniff at this opportunity of keeping the communication channels open. In other words, don't be choosy about what brings your friend to your door – or over-sensitive about the length of time it's taken him/her to consult you. Once you have listened to the problem (if it *is* a problem), do bear in mind that hindsight is useless. Listening to details of your friend's current situation, which is possibly an uncomfortable one, it is all to easy to say that if he/she hadn't gone into this partnership/agreed to provide for all the children/taken for granted that the kids would love their stepmother, stepfather or whatever, then he/she wouldn't be sitting here now being miserable. But that is hindsight: a fool-proof crystal ball in reverse. It won't do your friend any good to hear even a hint of 'I told you it would happen' – and, more important, he/she won't consult you again.

If the lone parent concerned is remarrying after being widowed, then your discretion must be greater still. No one wishes to speak ill of the dead, naturally, yet no one really wants to be honest about them either. It won't help if any approach made to you results in your giving chapter and verse on the dead partner's qualities, or if you start drawing tacit comparisons between the late husband/wife and the future one. Yes, you liked and respected the dead spouse (or, frankly, you didn't, or found it hard to get along with him/her). But now everyone wants to start again – and this includes *you*.

Advising step-parents

Someone you know intends to join a family (or, indeed, has already joined one) as a step-parent. What are your reactions? If you're their parent, will you become a *de facto* grandparent? Do you have any special responsibilities or obligations? What can you do to help? The new partner, with or without children, has to make his/her place in the existing family, whom you may not know well. He/she therefore needs support from:

- his/her partner (the parent)

- the family he/she is about to join

- you, as his/her friend or relative

Assistance from the first two, the partner and the family, might come slowly at first. The partner, hoping to acquire above all a husband or wife, could be more absorbed in the adult relationship than in the nitty-gritty of helping his/her spouse through the initial stages of what may feel like a rather strange family life. The children (and other family members) might not welcome a step-parent immediately, for a variety of reasons; one can't always expect a hero's welcome starting at the wedding reception! Apart from the children, there are other relatives – notably the grandparents, maternal and paternal – who may have doubts. All these things may leave the new partner somewhat short of support.

This is where you come in. Lead, and hope that others will follow. Back up your friend/relative in the early and sometimes difficult stages of joining the family; think positively about what he/she is trying to do. Even if you're concerned in case the step-parent should meet nothing but added worry and a heavier workload, try looking at it another way: these responsibilities, taxing though they may be, lead to greater maturity and tolerance. If you sense a practical difficulty – such as spare time being very short with a family to care for – then offer practical support, for instance helping out so that the couple can enjoy a break together. If asked for advice, whether on an emotional or a practical matter, give it freely and cheerfully. (Don't provide a sermon as well as a recipe when your daughter rings up for a recipe, just because you know it's for her husband and his three hungry kids!)

Should the family invite you to join in, do so with a good heart and an open mind. Children emerging from divorce or bereavement don't always behave very prettily, incidentally, so don't gasp with disbelief when you turn up to find two or more of them beating hell out of each other on a sofa while another sits in the corner quietly picking his nose. Don't frown with disapproval if they all appear to shuffle out of the room in a crab-like motion, going rather red and mumbling – or if they appear to cling, leech-like, to their fond parent, not letting go for about half an hour. They too have insecurities, but not being adults don't feel bound to dissemble. There is nothing personal in all this, so take any eccentricities you discover in good part. And in case you're wondering why no one comes across with a polite introduction, try to accept also that in this situation protocol is valueless.

If as a senior relative you wait for the children to behave 'nicely' towards you, showing due deference to their step-parent's mother/father or whatever, you may have to wait a long time. Make that important first contact *yourself*. And don't stop trying if it doesn't work immediately. At Christmas, remember everyone in the family; make a note of the children's birthdays and show that you know them. Costly presents or elaborate treats are unnecessary: a thoughtful card or small gift will do. Being remembered as part of your circle has more meaning than anything expensive and contrived. This is doubly important if the group concerned consists of two joined families: don't send cards or gifts to 'your' children without doing the same for the others.

Beware of falling into the 'lip-service' trap! It's no good telling all and sundry that your friend/relative is doing a 'splendid job with all those children' and then dropping a heavy hint that he/she must be a lunatic to have taken it on. And it is doubly useless if, having praised your friend/relative to others, you radiate disapproval and displeasure from every pore whenever you actually see the family. When you visit them it should not be merely as 'Jane's father', 'David's sister' or whatever, fiercely protecting your rather foolish relative who has chosen to marry into a family; you are there to be sociable with *everyone*. And, back once more to the children's behaviour: however many 'please' and 'thank you' opportunities may be missed, however offhand or rude you may think they are, try not to over-react. It's useless to chalk up misdemeanours on any kind of mental slate. And, temporarily comforting though it may be to talk to other friends or relatives about the children's odd ways, it only reinforces the negative thoughts you may have. Enough barriers exist in these complex relationships without your adding more.

Does all this sound impossible? If you can't see your way to making an honest effort, then step back. Allow yourself a bit more time to adjust and then see how you feel.

There is one rule which is very important here. If you feel that for whatever reason you just cannot accept the family as a whole or even just the new partner, don't go out of your way to encourage your friend/relative to see you on their own. Don't start being difficult, hinting that you don't want anyone else to come along. It is a very divisive practice. While there are immediate practical reasons against you always receiving the family en masse they can, with ingenuity, be overcome. For example, you may not be able to make free with meals on the grand scale, or overnight hospitality. Does your invitation have to include a meal? You can, you say, accommodate one person overnight, but not several – but who's talking about everybody staying with you? The next time you plan to entertain a few people – on some occasion calling for a party, perhaps – why not invite the family? Two adults and a few children among a larger gathering will make virtually no practical difference. Your contact with them will be easier, too, reducing the amount of one-to-one conversation you have with them, if this is something you find difficult.

Regardless of your feelings, and however well or badly you handle your meetings with the step-parent and the family concerned, moments of crisis are bound to arise when your friend/relative will approach you for help. He/she will appear upset and in need of a sympathetic ear. How do you intend to handle the situation? 'With sympathy, of course!' I can practically hear you shout back at me! That's a purely instinctive feeling; after all, you may have had serious misgivings about your friend's becoming involved in a stepfamily – and now here he/she is, crying on your shoulder. It is the easiest thing in the world to take your friend's part unreservedly, criticizing everyone else in the family and agreeing that the other partner is using him/her and that the children are unspeakable. Nevertheless, resist the temptation to do so. It's a trap – not one that is wittingly sprung, granted – but a trap just the same, which will lead to a whole new spiral of trouble. So keep away from it.

Be kind, by all means. Identify with your friend's problem while you put the kettle on or offer a drink – but keep both your minds on the job. For good or ill a commitment has been made to a parent and children. Assuming that it takes time for two adults to learn to live together harmoniously, how much longer must it take for a group whose number could be anything between three and ten assorted adults and children? Try to be objective; don't rush in and find your friend/relative right all along. Gently raise the subject of the children: don't they too have difficulties which they sometimes show in a rather brutal way? What about your friend's partner? Surely he/she is being pulled in several different directions, wanting to placate the children *and* do his/her best for a new partner? When your friend has cooled off – or cheered up – encourage him/her to go home and talk the problem over with the other partner. He/she can always ring you, or pop in again if the safety valve looks as if it is going to blow.

That is one way of dealing with a temporary crisis. Unconditional sympathy is quite another. Although you may think that to be totally on your friend's side is a positive attitude, it's not. It fills the unhappy step-parent with negative ideas, ranging from the viewpoint that all this is not his/her responsibility (very damaging) to the conviction that the whole venture is a ghastly mistake and, yes, you were quite right, he/she should never have become involved with this particular adult and set of kids in the first place. You will find your friend nodding his/her head and agreeing with you: he/she ought to have known it would cause nothing but trouble. That, if I may say so, is dynamite. Lavish sympathy – and the so-called benefit of hindsight on someone in this situation, and he/she will return home with all the ammunition required for one furious row.

You will fill your friend/relative with ideas that are far more positive if, having listened to whatever the problem is, you drop into his/her ear a few words of encouragement, such as: 'I admire you for doing this. *I* couldn't tackle it!' Not everyone is capable of taking on a ready-made family. This person, who is doing so, deserves praise for trying, however traumatic the experience might prove to be.

The common theme

Whatever your interest as a bystander, your role is essentially one of unobtrusive help and support. Everyone involved needs encouragement, and it is up to you to help supply it.

There is one aspect of being a bystander which some people forget – or prefer to. After a bit of a struggle they accept that their friend/relative has actually put his/her head in the noose, that he/she is a step-parent. But what will everyone else think? Acceptance of the situation (when necessary, in front of the family) followed by public martyrdom won't work. It should be remembered that there is nothing second-rate or shabby about this type of partnership or marriage; it is in no respect inferior to less complicated first-time marriages or subsequent ones where no children are involved. A parent and children are not defective because they have been through divorce or bereavement. Your friend/relative is not scraping the bottom of the barrel in marrying a parent; it doesn't imply that he/she couldn't have found someone more 'eligible'.

Help, love and support if you possibly can. It makes all the difference.

7

What happens if . . . ?

Here we shall discuss two situations which frequently arise: firstly, when arrangements between parents and children change, transforming a 'weekend' parent and step-parent into permanent ones; and, secondly, what can happen when two parents get together in the hope of forming one larger family.

1. They're staying – for good!

You are a couple getting to know each other and coping with visits from the family at weekends or in the holidays; then, possibly overnight, everything changes. For one good reason or another a child (or children) is unable to remain with one parent and has to move in with the other: which means you, in your home. If you are the step-parent yet were not closely involved as one before, now you certainly will be. If you are the parent, slightly unused to having the children around all the time, you will doubtless be very pleased to think that they will be under your roof again. But do spare a thought for your partner, especially if he/she (more likely to be 'she' here, as this situation often occurs when children who have lived with their mother make the move to live with dad, for whatever reason) knows little about coping with the family.

If you were to approach your partner and obtain absolutely honest replies to your views on having the children for good, you might be rather shocked:

Parent	Partner
'Of course they must live with us.'	'Why should they?'
'I don't see that they'll cause *that* much extra work.'	'Maybe not for you. But what about *me*?'
'It's their home too.'	'And it's *my* home!'
'It'll be great to have them.'	'Will it?'
'You don't mind – do you?'	'Yes, I mind like hell!'

66

There's a yawning gap between how a parent sees this and how his/her partner views the situation. Weekend stays and holidays are one thing — but to have the children permanently? Admittedly, the above scene is purely hypothetical and presents a somewhat exaggerated view of parental enthusiasm clashing with the step-parent's initial (and natural) reluctance. Let's re-run it, this time adding a little more compromise:

Parent	*Partner*
'The children need to live here. What do you think?'	'Why exactly? Explain what's happened.'
'Do you think you can cope?'	'I don't know. But perhaps I can if you help.'
'It is their home too. They spend quite a bit of time here already.'	'Yes. But I think of it as *our* home, at least most of the time.'
'I'm really looking forward to having them here.'	'I know. But don't rush me!'
'It's all rather sudden. Do you mind?'	'It is unexpected. But I'll do my best.'

The variations on this are endless – there are about as many opening dialogues as there are situations – but if you try to come together and work together the chances are that you'll get off to a reasonable start. What you can't help are the circumstances that bring the children to you. Unfortunately, there are times when children are shipped wholesale to the part-time parent's home without any warning. There are also occasions when a previous agreement is broken and a scheme to send a youngser to live with his dad at, say, sixteen, falls apart: the teenager makes his/her move ahead of schedule. As a parent you may be in a position of helplessness, relying entirely on the goodwill of your partner. And as a partner you may sympathize yet be unable to help feeling (particularly in the wake of an acrimonious divorce) the whole thing is some kind of conspiracy.

The nature of the arrangements made at the time of a divorce is such that they hinge almost entirely on the goodwill of the ex-partners, which means that whoever obtains custody must be as generous as he/she can to the partner who has not. Where joint custody is awarded a far greater chance exists of there being a real rapport between both parents. The trouble, of course, is that what works in the case of two or three under-tens may not provide the answer when the children reach twelve or fourteen or want to leave school. It can be impossible to bury the hatchet some years after a long and bitter battle has been fought in the courts – and to swallow one's pride sufficiently to admit that one or more of the children now really wants to live with Dad instead.

Whatever the background to the children's rather sudden materialization in your home, try to forget it if you possibly can. It is nothing to do with the children themselves, unless they are old enough to make a knowing choice. And if younger offspring engineered the decision (as can happen once Dad seems to have acquired a female partner), there may well be a valid reason for it which deserves close examination whether or not they actually end up living with you permanently.

To avoid a poor start it would be ideal if all the adults concerned could meet and discuss the change-over. This would do much to take the heat out of the situation and give each couple (where applicable) a better understanding of the reasons for it. Although communications are rarely good enough to allow this, it really would be the most sensible thing to do.

Parents

You have got what you wanted: after what may have been years of seeing your family in less than satisfactory circumstances, they are actually going to live with you. If this is a new arrangement which has been discussed with your former spouse, then fine: you should have had a chance to talk it over with your new partner and the situation may not be too fraught. If, however, you have had all this arranged for you — perhaps with a child turning up with a larger bag than usual and a brief to tell you that he/she isn't going home — then it's much more difficult. The shock will hit your partner hardest. He/she will have misgivings, certainly; but please don't take his/her feelings personally. Your partner knew all along (I hope!) that you were a parent and that though it seemed unlikely there was always a chance that this might happen. He/she understands the wider issues at stake: the children have a right to be happy and secure. And if this can be achieved in *your* home, then so be it. Your partner knows that you, as a parent, are pleased to have this chance. Yet this knowledge does not prevent a massive attack of nerves, nor does it automatically smooth the path of daily life. You are excited and pleased at the prospect of being a 'family' again. He/she may be worried to death about things you consider irrelevant, such as who takes the children to school – and who picks them up? Who goes on all the expeditions to find and buy clothing, shoes, things for school? Who finds the extra cash required to feed two more small mouths (or stoke up two ravenous teenagers)? How will the family manage in terms of room and privacy? All this might seem rather trivial set against the prospect of having your children back, but these could well be your partner's preoccupations. And since you have to work *together*, he/she needs support and some practical help. What you now think of as minor problems will eat away at the well-being of everybody concerned – so see to them. As has often been said before, small things are what stepfamily life is all about!

Partners

From being a step-parent, mainly at weekends and other periods when the family stay with you, you now have to make the transition to full-time responsibility. Depending on the circumstances that bring the children to your home, there may or may not be time for such a transition – so you will have to do the best you can.

While your partner, the parent, will accept the children without thinking about it, simply allowing them to come and live in your home if the occasion demands, for *you* it is very much a conscious decision. You are not to be blamed if you think it is all unfair; after all, the sudden change of plan may well be something you didn't ask for. (It may even be something you never thought about!) There is pressure on you to agree. If the children have to come without much warning, what kind of person will you appear to be if you say a firm 'no' to your partner? It is very much up to you to decide what kind of contribution you can make. It is probably in your own interest to accept gracefully, regardless of the chaos you think it will cause. Why? Because the chances are that even if you said 'no', the children would come in any case. And then all your refusal would achieve would be an enormous rift between you and your partner.

Try to see the situation from a point of view other than your own. What about your partner, for instance? He/she may be delighted at the thought of the children living with you both permanently, yet a little bewildered at first after what may have been a long period of seeing them only intermittently. He/she could already have enough on their emotional plate, having had to ask for your support or explain to you why the children appear to have materialized so suddenly.

You could have any number of anxieties, ranging from fears about your job (How much involvement are you expected to have with the children, and to what extent will this cut across a job whose responsibilities might not be compatible with term time and school holidays?) to fears about your relationship with your partner (lack of privacy, less time together, jealousy caused by the children claiming time, energy and attention which were previously 'yours'). It could be difficult to work out the nuts and bolts of the new regime, so very different will it be from living as a couple. You will have to talk over many of these matters with your partner, asking his/her advice about the children, picking their parent's brains in order, as it were, to get to know them better.

Meanwhile accept the fact that, temporarily, your partner and the children are at the top of the list.

Guidelines

• If you get an opportunity to discuss the children's projected change of home with *both* parents, then do so.

• Once the children are with you, talk over together (adults *and* children wherever possible) the things that affect your day-to-day life: meals, bedtimes, homework, help around the house and so on.

• Keep in close contact. The adults could be manipulated by

the children, who might be tempted to make the most of the fact that it's a new situation and there are *two* adults, one they may not know too well (plenty of opportunity for playing one off against the other!)

- Don't discourage the children from talking about the past, even if this presents problems. Encourage them to feel good about the parent they have just left. The two of you, parent and step-parent, will gain nothing by creating 'goodies' of yourselves and tacitly writing off the absent parent as a villain.

- However uncomfortable it may be intitially, or however much you feel the children are 'acting up', *never* do or say anything to give the impression that they will be shipped back to where they came from. It is the children's right to live with their parent; no great favours are being dispensed.

- Keep the situation (the one which brought the children to you, perhaps unexpectedly) quite separate from your basic relationship as adults: in other words, don't let some of the difficulties trick the two of you into thinking you dislike each other. If you argue about practical issues – work, money, lack of spare time or privacy and so on it is not so bad, providing you and your partner still like and sympathize with each other.

- Don't shut out the other parent. Even after the most dramatic blow-ups feelings will heal, and it will do no good for the now-absent parent to feel punished for the change-over.

- Don't be shy of asking for help! Approach STEPFAMILY, or someone you trust (a friend or clergyman, for instance). Contact the Marriage Guidance Council; or, as a first step, contact a local radio 'careline'.

- Enlist the help and support of schools, where appropriate. Make sure that you inform the children's teachers so that it is known that they now live with you. If previously you didn't receive school reports or notices of events for parents, make

sure you get them now. And ask if the other parent can
continue to receive information too.

- Bear in mind that what feels unfamiliar and uncomfortable
  now will soon become a great deal easier. The children are
  probably feeling rather lost too. It *does* get easier and
  pleasanter as you all get to know one another.

- Don't feel that the sudden arrival of an 'instant' family
  automatically precludes you from enjoying adult activities.
  If you attend a regular class, have a hobby or are used to
  inviting friends round frequently, carry on doing these
  things: you will need your outside sources of relaxation!

2. Two into one?

How do you get two families to coexist successfully under one
roof? 'With difficulty!' I have been told. At least the two adults
are both parents and as such likely to be aware of many of the
problems involved. Yet this fact alone is no guarantee that they
will succeed in curing some of the very unfamiliar ills which can
arise when two families merge. It is a case of ridding the
household of the 'his' and 'hers' (or 'yours' and 'mine') syndrome
– not to be achieved without consistent hard work.

Much depends on the families in question, their backgrounds
and the way each of them has done things in the past. Age comes
into it too, great disparities or similarities bringing their own
problems. For instance, how do older children (by which I mean
adolescents) react when expected to coexist with two relative
infants? Aren't they likely to feel miffed because the little ones
seem to get away with murder? And if the new arrangement
means that youngsters almost identical in age will now be living
in the same house, will they slug it out for supremacy?

The onus lies squarely on the adults concerned. They have to
work together, far more so than a 'normal' mum and dad, to keep
all channels of communication open. Of course there will be
sources of resentment: why, you may protest, should my children
be told off sharply while his/hers seems to get away with being
very naughty indeed? Loving someone else's children is not

something that comes automatically, particularly if you are still nursing your own in the aftermath of a divorce or loss of a parent. It is as well to rid yourself of this assumption straight away. While eventually you and your partner's children may strike up a deep friendship involving a great deal of mutual affection and respect, you can't expect to love them as you do your own. (Bystanders, please note: you may mean well when you say things like 'I'm sure you think of him/her just as your own', but though this is a worthy sentiment, things don't work that way.) There may be unexpected qualities in the relationship you have with your stepchildren, so that as a step-parent you occasionally get on better with a stepchild than with a natural one – yet there will always be a difference. Accept this from the outset and you will not waste time feeling guilty.

Jealousy in the family

Jealousy is a prominent feature of the stepfamily, and this is assuredly the case when two families join together. It is as if the jealousy transforms itself into a pernicious kind of ivy, hooking its tentacles round everyone involved. The adults may feel jealous when looking at each other's children, who are, after all, proof positive of each's previous marriage and sexual activity. The children may feel jealous of the new adult, occasionally wishing that he/she had never met mum or dad and come along to spoil things. Then they may well feel jealous of their ersatz brothers and sisters: invariably better off or in a better position regarding the adults in the household, less likely to be told off or punished, more favourably regarded and so forth. The rotten thing about jealousy is that it is so totally unacceptable: such a basic, brutal and nasty emotion can, we say, never be justified. It's what a toddler feels about a dear little baby brother or sister, isn't it – so surely a child of ten or an adult can do better than that? Yet jealousy is something we never outgrow, and the form it takes does not become any more acceptable with the passage of time. Quite the reverse: an adult suffering from its pangs gets a very definite thumbs-down from better-adjusted friends.

It is pointless to try to sweep jealousy under the carpet in a stepfamily. It might even be the one thing you all feel and wish you didn't: a possible strength (if admitted to) rather than a weakness. Trying to push the feeling aside will do no good whatsoever; you have got to face it and live through it. The following suggestions may help you to avoid some of the difficulties.

In the home

First of all, there is the question of housing. Are you expecting to house both families in one or other of the homes where the children have grown up? It may be worth considering a new home for everyone. Although moving house is expensive, it could prove a good investment: a great deal of misery can be caused when the home one family thinks of as its own suddenly becomes 'invaded'. A dispute which is purely territorial can be very awkward and, as with many other so-called minor issues in stepfamily life, festers within weeks or months. Expecting one adult partner to share what was once the family home with others is hard enough; think how difficult that could seem to two or three children!

If the combined family has a limited age range it should be possible, at least in theory, to arrive at broad rules which apply to everyone. If all the children concerned know there are set times for meals, homework, going to bed and so forth, that will reduce the difficulty. Admittedly, one group may lose out initially: free-thinking youngsters unaccustomed to being asked to be in bed by a certain time or to make a regular habit of how they do homework etc. might view the enforcement of a new regime as downright draconian. Yet a routine which permits the family as a whole to get through all the work involved and enjoy their free time will benefit everyone in the long run.

As an aside, I must say how this worked out in our family. We did not have two groups of children, but for various reasons we had to impose certain rules when one of my husband's offspring suddenly opted to live with us permanently. While I realized the importance of setting a more or less regular pattern, I doubted whether the child in question would submit to it. In the event he did, willingly. It seems that there was something in our plan which added to his overall sense of security, almost as if the constraints we imposed made for a greater feeling of his permanence with us, a feeling that he really did belong. The most important thing is to ensure that *both* groups of children are treated the same: it will not work if one group has to abide by the rules while the other is allowed to get off scot-free.

This brings us back to the notion of 'his' and 'hers'. It is the easiest thing in the whole world to protect your children, if you are a parent. Two parents joining their families may quite unthinkingly seek to protect their own children by encouraging each set of offspring to refer only to their natural parent. Such parents may feel that to begin with it could be hurtful for their children to have instructions and advice dished out to them by the other partner, with the result that they find ways round certain situations, putting off the day when each child will have to deal directly with his/her step-parent. As long as children feel it is possible to take instructions from their own parent while ignoring the wishes of the other adult, there will be problems: it just won't be possible to get all the children in the family living along the same lines. Quarrels and ill feeling will blow up from nowhere, whether it's over which TV programme to watch, who helps with the washing-up, who can or can't go out depending on how much homework has been done, or whatever. It is most important that adults should overcome their fears as quickly as they can. The partner you married (or live with) is not likely to harm your children. If that person is able to deal with his/her own family, why shouldn't he/she take an active role in helping with yours? Why should any rational, intelligent adult have this fear of their partner pitching in?

We all fear what we don't know. As a parent, you know your own children (at least you think you do, though as they grow up this becomes less certain!) and, allowing for the possible stresses of divorce or bereavement, manage to deal with them from day to day. Their tears and tantrums, moods and silences are familiar to you; even if they infuriate you, most of their eccentricities are known. But what about your stepchildren? You know them socially; you know their parent rather well – so well, in fact, that you live in the same house and sleep in the same bed. But what about the moment when the crunch comes? If you tell one of them to do something, request their help or insist on a point of routine, what kind of response do you get?

Bearing in mind your own likely inhibitions where another's children are concerned, it is easy to transfer this attitude to your thinking about your own. *You* may be hesitant about dealing directly with your stepchildren and so readily assume that your partner feels the same way. And besides, it is easier, at least for the first few weeks or months, to avoid confrontations. But when does the 'honeymoon' end?

Points to remember

- However embarrassing or difficult it may be, don't prolong the 'hands off' period with stepchildren for too long. Take the chance of direct involvement with them, *not* confining parental advice and duties to your children alone. Better still, talk the subject over with your partner so that both sets of children become well aware that it's not just 'their' parent who will be dealing with them.

- Think carefully about sleeping arrangements, the sharing of rooms and so forth. It is easily done but better avoided to have stepchildren feeling even slightly done down because the 'other' children seem to have the lion's share of room and facilities. Youngsters are more touchy than adults give them credit for.

- Education can be a difficult one. What do you do when two families converge with one fee-paying faction versus one state-educated? If you have both families before decision-making time it's obviously easier, but decisions have to be made which are fair to all. Whichever child comes of age first as far as changing schools is concerned, make the decision then on the basis of the two or three more who will eventually be doing the same. At all costs avoid a situation in which one or two children are privately educated and the rest are not. Even if the ex-partner (by which I mean the absent parent) or grandparents try to swing the decision by promising cash for fees, accept only if this means that all the children will still receive similar schooling.

- Stay as calm as you can when non-sibling rivalry sets in. It's a great wrecker of hopes for the family, but it can and will lessen. Above all, keep at the back of your mind the fact that two adolescents from different families who compete like mad for virtually everything could in fact be a lot friendlier than you bargain for. When a common sanction is being imposed or a common directive given for both children to work harder at school/do their homework/put in honest effort for exams and so on, this is often a great unifier.

- Very obvious, but very necessary: just like virtually every other pair at the head of a family, you should always tell the same tale and not be tempted to alter the rules for one or other set of children. The family will be ruthless in their 'divide and rule' policy and will soon implement it unless they know that both adults are in agreement.

- Discourage the 'separate camps' idea in any friends or relatives whom you see. Try to get the message across to grandparents or other relatives that the family is now four children or whatever, not just, say, one or two as it was before. A card or small gift, enquiries about school, and a genuine interest shown in *all* the children are most constructive and far preferable to relatives singling out 'their' part of the group.

- Don't over-react to your stepchildren's behaviour. It is well known that the most innocent pastimes irritate a step-parent like mad. While your kids may make a noise and wreck the place, your stepchild's (often minimal) disruption can appear a hundred times more difficult to bear. Just take a deep breath and remind yourself of this. You *will* get used to your partner's children – a process which won't be aided by your regularly hitting the roof. Remind yourself that children occasionally like to feel hard done by – and don't feed that tendency.

- Don't waste time on guilt because you don't love your stepchildren – or perhaps don't even like them. All step-parents assume that if they can't love their 'instant' family they (the adults, not the children!) must be defective. Why struggle for parental love when a friendly adult interest is a better base to build on?

- Find and keep up an outside pastime or hobby that will keep you sane. Don't give up the things you do just because of your increased family commitments. (Even your own children won't thank you for what you gave up supposedly for their benefit.)

- When problems, if any, supervene from your ex-partner, don't let them fester. Whatever the source of anxiety, major or minor, talk to your current partner and/or family about it: the general process of amalgamation will not be helped by a guerrilla attack taking place on the edge of the family.

- Advice that is repeated but no less valid for that reason: don't be shy of asking for help. STEPFAMILY welcomes all enquiries and new members, and it is surprising how much better you can feel just knowing that there are many others in a similar situation. Feelings can run very high at times, and you could feel at risk of harming a child/children in the family, so approach someone else before the risk becomes too great.

We all have good days and bad days. On good days we adults radiate benevolence and regard with interest the strange assortment of individuals who now populate the home. On bad days it's a monumental effort to drag oneself out to work, especially if part of the money earned is to be spent on 'their' school fees. With a frank and open approach, as much consistency as can be achieved and a generous effort on the part of everyone involved, the composite family can be a good place to live. But until you feel that good, don't feel *too* guilty if you occasionally wish you'd married that ideal man or woman, the childless orphan!

8

Pitfalls and pleasures

Another chronicle of what can go wrong? Yes, I am afraid so. A firm believer in relaying the bad news first, I put the cart before the horse yet again, cataloguing the possible disasters before telling my disbelieving readers that there *are* pleasant surprises ahead!

The pitfalls are to do with the children's reactions to stepparents and to their new situation in general: the disheartening episodes and tendencies you witness which sometimes leave you too appalled to know what to do, especially if you don't have children of your own.

Jealousy in the children

Endemic in stepfamilies and accountable for much strange behaviour in children whom you so dearly hope will settle into a 'new' family, jealousy manifests itself in the way they shout or go deathly silent, cling to a parent or reject everyone and generally do their utmost to put the new adult partner off. Why *should* children be so dog-in-the-mangerish?

It may not be obvious at first, but children can entertain some fairly colourful fancies about their future when parents divorce or in the period following bereavement. What happens if their parent, the one they are now living with, takes off and finds a new partner not, as an adult would see it, to form a relationship with that person, but specifically to have more babies? To a child this implies that he or she will be left behind, and there is a curiously consoling pleasure to be derived from the 'Orphan Annie' perspective. It can be years before the child realizes this was unlikely – just imagine the suffering that goes on in the meantime!

What makes a child close in physically on his/her parent? Why should a child spend an entire weekend sitting on Mum's or Dad's knee, following him/her around everywhere (even to the loo!) and generally seeing to it that the adult in question has no chance of doing anything but remain in close contact? Right again: it's jealousy, making the child stake out nothing less than a territorial claim on the parent's person.

You may not know it, but as the interloping adult – however relaxed you may think you are, however detached you may tell yourself to be – you represent a giant-sized threat to the child. You are going to take his/her parent, and the jealousy hurts physically. It's hard to tolerate your being in the same room, turning up (again!) at mealtimes, insinuating yourself all round the house. Small wonder that would-be partners find it practically impossible, at first, to manage spending a night with the parent. And what partner does not feel a similar jealousy? Just as you thought you might have five minutes alone for your own much-wanted and much-needed physical contact, here's the child again, wrapping itself firmly round the lover you can't seem to get your hands on!

If you're the parent, you may find this embarrassing. But accept it, regardless of however demonstrative or otherwise your child (or children) has been before. Don't single out your son or daughter with scoldings to 'stop it', or admonish him/her for being 'babyish'. Just for now, that physical contact provides valuable reassurance in the face of something he/she fears.

As an actual or potential step-parent you could feel that one or more of the children has a definite 'down' on you. I had that feeling in a big way when introduced to my prospective stepfamily. Admittedly, with five children in the picture the prospect was rather daunting, but one of them in particular made it quite clear. There was not contact at all between us: no conversation, no shared activity, no chance to get any closer – nothing. This state of affairs persisted for two years, during which I was certain the whole thing was highly personal. Abuse I could have endured better. That, at least, would have been some gesture, even a hostile one – but *this*? There is something about a silent child which makes adult efforts look and sound extemely silly; whatever you try, you look and sound a complete fool. The ice was finally broken when a holiday loomed on the horizon: there was space in the car and in a flat for one more person, and the erstwhile silent non-joiner took it. After two weeks away from home, we had achieved some sort of relationship – and it has prospered ever since.

The important point is that there is rarely a personal element, however unpleasant the atmosphere may be. The children are not rejecting *you*; they are fending off the future. They don't know what life will be like if you join the family, and temporarily they may prefer to cling jealously to the surviving or custodial parent and their memories of the past. Bystanders feeling a need to comment might thoughtlessly tell you that if only you were younger/older, had children yourself, etc. it would all be easier, but that isn't necesarily the case. Suppose the children *did* get rid of you? They would then perhaps dispatch the next contender, and the next, and so on. Unless you have made it harder for the children, or somebody else has intervened to ensure that you won't get off to a good start, this is a process which has to be lived through. The children cling tenaciously to (a) the surviving or custodial parent, (b) the absent parent, whom they obviously don't see as often, and (c) the past, when they had two 'normal' parents. Your coming into the picture throws them off balance and just tightens their grip. Things can and will change.

Loyalty

There is a vital factor to be considered when trying to understand children's loyalties, especially after a divorce: quite simply, the past, with all its difficulties and the divorce or bereavement which caused the current situation must *not* be swept under the carpet. It seems a strange thing to advocate, in this book dedicated to a family's fresh start – but there it is. Well-meaning friends and relatives will be the first to remind everyone that it is a new beginning: little Jane/Johnny must do all he/she can to make their 'new daddy' or 'new mummy' feel at home. But what about the old one? Why should the children of a widowed mum or dad be expected to embrace a 'new' parent when they haven't yet sorted out all the feelings they need to live through when a natural parent dies? To put pressure on a child to forget the past and wholeheartedly accept the present is a short-sighted pastime; it is also an insult to a child's intelligence. We all see right through it when a careless television producer prolongs the life of a character in a series or serial simply by substituting a new actor. We are led to believe, on the screen, that the character is just as it was before.

But how on earth can we swallow that when a new person emerges looking, sounding and acting quite differently from the first?

In a stepfamily situation, the child knows from the word go that this person is *not* 'Mummy' or 'Daddy' – so why should anyone push him/her into believing it? (My own theory is that it is easier and less embarrassing for outsiders.) Children need a chance to talk about the past so that they can live through all the feelings it evokes and progress to the next stage: the phase where their existing parent is married to somebody else. Cut that evolution short, and you will be in trouble. When you, as a parent or step-parent, feel that you are in close enough contact with the child not to appear nosy, try to let him/her talk about the past, their life before the divorce or the days after the funeral. When the past is out in the open it can't be quite so fearful/glamorous/desirable, and the future looks less formidable. Above all, make the children feel good about what has happened, if at all possible. How many youngsters grow into adults thoroughly convinced that their parents' divorce was all *their* fault – but have never had an opportunity to talk it over with anyone? As a step-parent, you could provide a very good sounding-board. Many children find that trying to unravel some of what has happened with a parent is traumatic; they become involved in an argument with raised tempers and forcefully expressed views before they know what to do. If you are sympathetic and able to achieve that balance of interest which is free of morbid curiosity, you could do your stepchildren a real service by listening quietly to them.

This will also give you an insight into some of their strange loyalties. On the face of it, why should some small change in their lives meet with such fierce opposition? Why should a shift of mealtime or new rule not to play outside after eight o'clock create an international incident? You will soon realize that it is not the detail which is significant here but the principle. Altered arrangements may be taken as an erosion of the way things were done in the past: the children may feel that if they go on at this rate, allowing the fabric of their daily lives to be nibbled at by an interfering new adult, there will soon be nothing left. Changes can easily be made slowly and with tact. This will be a lot less difficult for you – and it won't stretch the children's loyalties too far initially.

The next time you hear about the absent or dead parent – how lovely he/she is/was, how clever, how amusing and so forth – you will scream, or strangle whoever said it. If this really gets on your nerves, talk about it with another adult, perhaps your partner; don't vent your frustration on the child. This is a necessary process and must be allowed to work itself out.

Much as you may occasionally want to shout, 'Don't be daft! She's useless!' or whatever the appropriate comment is, please don't. You will only fuel the flames and ensure further bouts of ear-bending on the subject of your rival. The child of divorced parents wants to believe, above all, that *both* of them are still concerned and loving. Contradiction by the interloper – you – will result in nothing but tears, even if you really suspect the child's view of the absent or dead parent to be a defective one. When the child becomes mature he/she may draw his/her own conclusions, perhaps admitting, very reluctantly, that the parent in question did let him/her down or wasn't as caring as he/she could have been. This revelation comes soon enough. Don't demolish their emotional castles in the air.

Attention-seeking

In a stepfamily, or a potential one, it seems to a child as if there is suddenly far less attention to go round. Mum or Dad doesn't bother with him/her so much now that 'he' or 'she' is in the house – and, anyway, this person goes out of their way to make sure that the child is ignored, don't they? Matters can be worse, with two adults up to their necks in difficulties so that for a time the child seems unable to get much change out of either of them, finding himself/herself permanently fobbed off with adult worries which are always about the same boring old things: money, jobs, access and so on. So what is the best way of making absolutely sure that you get a parent's attention?

One sure-fire way is to do everything the parent finds infuriating. A good all-out attempt rarely fails, and when you see the heightened colour and look of annoyance and become aware that activities are temporarily suspended – even if it's to deliver a mis-aimed clout round the ear – you've succeeded.

To a step-parent, this all looks very odd. It seems as though the child is doing his/her level best to sabotage the adults' relationship. Yet this isn't necessarily so; the child is actually saying, loud and clear, 'I'm here – look at *me*!'

So now we know where attention-seeking comes from and a small part of the reason for its existence, what do we do about it? First, don't ignore it. What may provide a short-term measure stacks up a heap of trouble in the longer term. As a parent, it might be a good idea to be honest with yourself when thinking about the time you spend with the children. On the face of it, you're always 'around' – but do you spend time talking with them? It is very helpful if cries for attention (like any other pressing problem, such as questions on sex, which tend to be asked in supermarkets!) are met promptly. Let the children talk, even about what seem trivial things: there amid the assortment will probably lie what is bugging them. How many times do you think the hottest issue is barely mentioned – apart from, say, when the child skips out of the car to dash into school, leaving you thinking, 'What was all that about?' A forgotten promise to talk it over when there's time is worse than useless. However uncomfortable a conversation might be, better to tackle the problem as it arises if you possibly can. What may be a small thing to you, an adult, can, if not aired promptly, mushroom to enormous proportions, causing real trouble.

Problems at school

Difficulties in the home are one thing. Tackling problems and coming into contact with *outside* organizations – clubs, schools, authorities, firms, etc. – are quite another. Added to the angst of getting Junior off the hook (or not) is the whole business of having yourselves viewed as a stepfamily in public. Although an extreme measure, it is hardly surprising therefore that some stepfamilies actually decide to *move* after having a confrontation of some sort or other with the outside world. To picture a family seeking a new home and new schools is rather pathetic, but it does happen.

As a step-parent you could take issues involving school to be the responsibility of your partner and not your own; yet they are your responsibility too. A step-parent's reluctance to tackle the powers that be may stem from the hurdle of introducing yourself as a step-parent in the first place. Why let yourself in for the knowing glance and whispered comment, just audible as you leave the school office? Establishments where the staff should know better still display an amazing amount of ignorance where stepfamilies are concerned.

When it fell to me to discuss my stepchild's progress and/or problems at school, after a swift change-over from one parent's household to the other's, I had the distinct impression that it was *I*, not the child, who was getting the dressing-down! And, as an ex-schoolteacher, I can assure you I was not being unduly sensitive. On the face of it, the staff concerned may well have felt rather hostile. A boy disappears for the vacation with no evidence of a major change in circumstances. He reappears for the new term, brought to school by a strange (and very young) woman who claims that (a) the pupil is now living with his father and that (b) she is responsible for him during Father's absence, which could last for most of the term. No reassuring documentary evidence to prove this – and who is she, anyway? Ah, Father's girlfriend! (Any number of constructions could be placed on that nebulous title.) Whether any of this is actually voiced, it is unlikely, with luck, that a step-parent will be given such a doubting reception. It is worth explaining the circumstances as best you can, without being drawn on the finer detail, just in case someone, somewhere is merely curious. There are, of course, occasions where you just can't win. A stepmother, especially a relatively young one, will be viewed as a lightweight; stepfather, as the villain of the piece, the heartless Lothario with whom the mother is selfishly enjoying herself.

When visiting school to discuss a problem, first explain briefly who you are (the school records may not show your name, and this can be confusing). Next, remember that whatever may be inferred, you are there in the capacity of adult responsible for that particular child. Then enquire precisely what has happened and whether or not a punishment has been set. If the case is a more serious one request an appointment with the form tutor or headmaster, making sure that (a) the parent will also be able to go along if possible and (b) the whole matter is thoroughly discussed at home in the meantime to prevent any embarrassing surprises in front of the school staff. Thank the person you see for bringing the matter to your attention, collect the erring child (if he/she hasn't already escaped) and make your exit with as much dignity as possible. You may find that since you are not the child's natural parent a teacher may either clam up or go into overdrive, acting on the misinformation that step-parents are rarely over-sympathetic towards the children in their care; if possible, stop a fluent account of all the misdeeds before it starts. If you are able to handle this type of episode, you deserve to be congratulated as a much-maligned step-parent who has acted with calm and authority.

Back home, the full inquiry might prove tougher than the brush with school. Play it by ear, hoping that if parent and child prefer to talk together in private they will do so productively, without omissions. Don't be tempted to force a confidence. However upset or embarrassed you may be feeling after your encounter with an irate member of staff, don't take your feelings out on the child, staging a full interrogation on the way home.

All defence mechanisms will be working, and you risk a great deal of unpleasantness because the child, already exposed before you in an unfavourable light, will be poised for the counter-attack. If you, possibly over-excited yourself, try to prise information out of him/her, tempers will be raised, angry insults traded and damage done: not a good prelude for a calm discussion later with Mum or Dad. No one will achieve much if Junior shouts the odds about 'him' or 'her' and their probing in the car on the way home. If information is volunteered, fine; otherwise, don't force things. The whole business of owning up to a problem at school or defending oneself against an unfair accusation is a complex one that can dredge up all manner of strange feelings.

If the entire episode takes place between parent and child without the step-parent being involved, then so be it. Later, when everybody is feeling more comfortable with one another, it could be that you are the one the children tell first – even if only to use you as a barometer of their parent's reaction. This isn't devious; it's a compliment. However irritating and uncomfortable such occasions may be, when your step-child is at odds with authority in general, don't get the issue out of proportion, allowing what may be a fairly trivial incident to cause rows which include everyone, from child and parents to visiting relatives and the budgie. Don't let a breach of the rules become a breach of the peace.

Lack of support from your partner

Here I refer mainly to that isolated feeling a step-parent can experience if his/her efforts in the family are not backed up by the partner, the child's natural parent. The subject has been discussed elsewhere in this book (see pp. 26–30), but because it can have such a devastating effect it is worth mentioning again. If you are a step-parent, whether on an occasional, a part- or a full-time basis, why on earth should your partner, the child's mum or dad, fail to lend support to your requests/ideas/wishes in connection with the family? On a really bad day you may think it's for a million reasons, the principal ones being that you're not loved or appreciated and that your partner prefers to ignore you in order to lavish attention on the children. One word from you, and they all do as they like, with Mum or Dad uttering not a single syllable in your defence. You feel more than a little stupid, and if your feelings are left to fester they will turn to silent resentment. You will dissociate yourself from the lot of them – and who can blame you?

Am I being melodramatic in stating that lack of support from one's partner can have devastating effects? I don't think so. Even in ordinary families, whose problems are as a rule less complex, parents who fail to pull together can end up in trouble. A teenage friend of mine had what I thought were the best, most liberal parents in the world. Mummy ruled the roost during the nursery and early school days because Daddy was rarely there. Come the age of reason, with healthy intellectual development flowering in the two children, Daddy reappears.

Starting at a magic moment in their early teens, the new regime seemed simplicity itself. They bowed to Mummy's rule when they were small – but now they're mentally equipped to choose, aren't they? Needless to say, Mummy and Daddy had quite different views on certain issues which arose within the family. Adolescents brought up in this sophisticated environment were surely capable of choosing wisely between the two 'deals' on offer – but were they? I may have envied my friend's short-lived liberty, but I don't now envy all the insecurities which that system bred.

And in a stepfamily, things can be far worse. There is no substitute for the old-fashioned advice to 'start as you mean to go on'. The only problem, of course, is that in most stepfamilies we haven't a clue as to the right way to start; we simply have to fumble through in the hope that our intuition will guide us to some of the answers.

Janette suspected she would have problems when faced with the volatile set-up of her fiancé Daniel and his two sons. There was a fair amount of to-ing and fro-ing, the children landing regularly in Janette's lap as soon as their mother realized Janette and Daniel were living together. She had little experience of children and no family of her own; she was also relatively very young to cope with the situation, though she did the best she could. She soon sensed that the boys needed security and a modicum of discipline to make up for some of the disruptions, and was confident that Daniel would back her up – but he didn't. Situations arose at home where Daniel avoided confrontation with his sons, thereby also avoiding lending Janette his support. She was forced to go it alone, and became worried about some of the trouble the boys got into, especially when this began to occur outside the home. The situation was no longer simply that of a woman wishing her partner to side with her in some domestic skirmish: Janette was aware of certain serious problems which had to be contained. She felt there was an urgent need for straight talking and outside help. Daniel, on the other hand, felt that things would blow over and tended to play down the difficulties, using his own influence to get his sons out of trouble rather than approaching one of the many authorities trained for the job.

Janette's ensuing illness could have been coincidental or a direct effect of the enormous stress she had begun to feel. She was no longer able to exert herself as she had done, and meanwhile the situation with the boys ran out of control. Daniel, by this time appalled, was not really able to face up to its gravity, and today, some years after the initial difficulties, both young men are away from home. Janette has not fully recovered, but she does not feel embittered; she regrets the fact that she and Daniel were unable to work together to retrieve her stepsons.

The problems outlined above are serious ones, and I am not saying that just because adults may fail to support each other in a bid to get stepchildren to co-operate the effects need necessarily be so dramatic. Yet there are any number of situations which are capable of escalating into something nasty. It is the principle of two adults pulling together which is vital; a division at home over something quite simple, with children being given plenty of latitude to do exactly as they please, will soon lead them to believe that outside the home – at school, college, work, etc. – they can do the same thing.

If you're a step-parent, it might help to try to put yourself in your partner's place. What is it that is stopping you from echoing the other adult's requests?

- Fear of confrontation. Particularly very early on, it seems the most desirable thing in the world to keep everything sweet and peaceful. Mum's or Dad's voice raised to join that of the step-parent can result in a shouting match all round, something most of us dread.

- Guilt. This spreads in all directions and is potentially very damaging. The natural parent, seeing his/her partner dealing with the children, can feel that none of this (divorce/remarriage/unsettled atmosphere, however temporary/unsettled children) would ever have happened if only something (attributable to them) had not gone wrong. If the partner is having a tough time getting used to the family, this again is a source of guilt for the parent.

- Loyalty becomes stretched beyond normal limits, with the natural parent wondering how on earth he/she can be loyal to both children and the new spouse. Small wonder that at crucial moments it's almost impossible to know which way to jump!

- There is a natural reluctance to face certain unpleasant incidents which tend to crop up in stepfamilies. If, as a parent, you see your children intermittently or are in the process of getting used to them all over again because of a sudden change in arrangements made following divorce, you may be unpleasantly surprised to note that they have become antisocial. You may disapprove of the way your ex-husband/ wife has dealt with important areas over the last few years. It may be comforting (if unrealistic!) now and then to lay the blame squarely in that quarter, but the fact remains that you don't like having to admit – even to yourself – that the behaviour of your growing family might not be what you had visualized. In such circumstances, of course, a parent will avoid a possible step-parent versus stepchildren confront- ation in the mistaken belief that avoiding the problem, at first in the short term and them indefinitely, is the answer. It isn't; it's just a cop-out. Yet facing up to this is not easy.

As a step-parent I rely heavily on my husband's support and have done so in all the years I have known his family. Even though it wasn't easy to broach the subject early on, we did talk about occasional problems as they arose, and decided that we would always try to 'tell the same tale' wherever possible.

The reluctant step-parent

Not such a sinister title as it sounds. Step-parents tend, by nature and circumstance, to be reluctant – only a lunatic would plunge him or herself *willingly* into grappling with someone else's children! But what happens when, against all expectations you, the parent, discover that your new partner is helping you out rather less than you'd hoped?

This a very difficult subject to talk about: within seconds there are hurt cries of 'I took them on, didn't I?', and arguments are very near the surface. On the face of it, your partner (the step-parent) did take on you *and* the family. He/she entered into this curious bargain, a marriage bringing with it more responsibilities than rights, and sooner or later it's time to convert the paper contract into a living one. But for some people it's just not as easy as that. It takes time and patience for a new step-parent to adjust, particularly if he/she does not have children. And even if he/she is a parent already, think how hard it may be for your partner to have to deal with your kids while seeing his/her own less frequently.

There are thousands of reasons for this reluctance. The children who appeared quite charming on short acquaintance might now start acting like monsters, secure in the knowledge that their best behaviour is no longer required. The courtship phase of your relationship – if you had one! – may now have to give way to the real nitty-gritty of daily life, which isn't nearly so much fun. External pressures, in the form of difficulties at work, the threat of redundancy or the continuing depression of unemployment, can throw a new step-parent off balance. Relatives and friends can be less than helpful, particularly if they are not sufficiently enlightened to accept the family as a whole rather than just champion their friend and be on guard for the first problem to come along. The new step-parent can be as insecure and doubting as any child, the problem being, of course, that an adult has far less of an excuse for showing this or admitting to it openly. Marriage is difficult enough in the early days – what must it be like when you feel as if you've 'married' not just one person but a whole bunch?

If many of the possible problems have been thought about and discussed beforehand, it helps. But nothing except honest effort will ever bridge the 'idea gap' which exists between the knowledge that you're supposed to be a working and supportive partner and the acceptance and practical execution of the job. And an honest effort is needed from as many quarters within the family as possible: no step-parent will slog it out alone once he/she becomes dimly aware that there is zero support from the adult partner and no attempt being made elsewhere for everyone to learn to live together. An early start with plenty of enthusiasm will soon give way to a less exuberant period, followed by a rather sullen patch as resentment sets in – and from then on it's downhill all the way.

Most reluctant step-parents find that marriage or permanent residence in their stepfamily is far worse, initially at least, than in their most lurid nightmares. Everything is chaotic: the house is full of angry rows, hysterical giggling – or else stony silence. The kind, attractive individual they married is now examined at close quarters and found to be deeply disturbed – or so it seems. What turns this perfectly acceptable individual into one capable of entirely unpredictable behaviour, cracking perfectly appalling jokes to make the sulking kids laugh, waxing lyrical over the new husband/wife's latest achievement (again in an attempt to jolly the family along) and generally behaving like a prize idiot?

Time and patience are well worth it, because even the most hesitant step-parent will become more confident if allowed the chance. If your partner is unsure in his/her dealings with the family, it is up to you to take the lead. If you are disappointed because things are not going as swimmingly as you'd hoped, try to conceal some of this feeling: the last thing a slow starter needs is a dose of guilt too early on in the process.

If you are a step-parent, whatever your degree of involvement with your partner's children, you would be wise to accept the role promptly. By this I do not mean that you should plunge in with a wild burst of enthusiasm (which will alarm everyone), but I would stress that any mental preparation on your part is never wasted. Even if you see your partner's children once a month or less, don't shirk the step-parent role and its responsibilities. Early accept-ance, even just in your own mind, of the fact that you are now a step-parent will lead in the end to a far easier acceptance of all the effort which will be asked of you.

Pleasures

Not without relief, I now list some of the perks. If you can survive the initial stage, you will arrive at the pleasant part. Please believe that you can and will get there. If, like me, you are the kind of person who expects nothing and is then pleasantly surprised when something turns up, you are at an advantage – that is not such a bad way of tackling step-parenthood!

After what seems a lifetime of monosyllabic hostility, your stepchild(ren) may actually ask you for help. The request may well be phrased in a most off-putting and casual manner calculated, it seems, to meet with your refusal. But please accept and comply. Whether it's checking homework, giving a lift into town, putting up a friend for the night or doing some other favour, accept the chance gladly. Consider it an opportunity offered to *you* and not *your* granting a favour to *him/her*.

If the approach is less than charming, why can't the child ask in a more attractive way? Surely, if he/she really wanted your help, he/she would appear a bit keener? Not necessarily. You have no time to argue about the niceties of the approach; it has been made, which is all that matters. You were possibly asked in a way that pointed at your refusal largely because this is what the child expected. If you knock the child back, you won't be hurting him/her too badly. If, however, you were asked nicely, it is likely that the child was very much hoping for your instant agreement. How hurt might he/she have then been by a flat refusal –or, even worse, a few minutes of cat-and-mouse play before you finally agreed to do as asked?

During the difficult period of adjustment when child is getting used to Mum or Dad's new partner, defences are fully on the alert and working. So if you the step-parent suddenly get an opportunity to improve the quality of your contact with the child, you are wise to grab it; there could be more, once the ice is broken. On a bad day you may feel that it's one step forward followed by several back – but it's the step forward that really counts.

It is also a pleasure to feel you're becoming a member of the family. Your birthday is remembered – and not necessarily with a card hastily bought by Dad on the kids' behalf. I am touched anew when Mother's Day comes round every year, though as a step-mother I do not for one minute expect any token on this day reserved for 'real' mothers. My gratitude and delight wipe out some of the early difficulties, I can assure you. You could be asked to go along to a school play or sports function; one of the children might ask you how something is done, such as programming the home computer or making curry. Eventually one of the family might come to you with news they need to get across to their parent or for an opinion on a potentially controversial subject – before they confront Mum or Dad. You could be asked to go swimming, or to a match or film – not just because there's no other adult to take the kids.

Even before you realize progress is being made, someone outside the family might remark to you how well the children look, or how good some of their school work is becoming, or even how much more sociable they sometimes appear to be. The person who gives the compliment deserves praise for showing a positive attitude. And you value their kind remarks – rightly – because whatever he or she is drawing attention to is more than likely to be genuine.

The pleasures of step-parenthood are small and hard-won. It is significant that problems take far longer to describe than rewards, which glow only dimly at the end of a very long, dark tunnel. But while problems need close attention, energy and time to solve, pleasures call for no analysis. If you keep any kind of diary, however erratically, record the pleasures, never the problems: it will make positive and encouraging reading. The few dates where some small measure of progress is recorded will cheer you up on another day when you might be feeling a bit miserable. Alternatively, reading a catalogue of family fights and mis-demeanours will do absolutely nothing for your morale.

What is your goal, as you join a family – or what was it when you started out? It is reasonable to suppose that your initial aim was a rather pretty picture: a happy couple surrounded by happy (well-disciplined and compliant!) children, living what looks to be a charmed live. Yet the goal diminishes once the realities of step-parenthood take hold. Constant compromise becomes the norm. If the whole picture fails to materialize, then you settle for one small piece at a time. You never lose sight of your goal – nor should you – but it remains what it is, an ideal. Meanwhile, you accept the small pleasures that time brings. It is unrealistic to expect instant affection all round, with you the step-parent basking at the heart of things, but it is possible for there to be friendship and respect once everyone starts to feel more comfortable together. If this sounds rather tame and trite, I make no apologies: the means to this end are far from tame. It takes guts, self-confidence, tenacity and an outsize sense of humour to take on a stepfamily. One of the most unexpected rewards comes later, when you look back and realize what you're capable of.

9

Room For One More?

You have taken on a stepfamily and are now wondering whether or not to set the seal on your new partnership by having a child of your own. This question is crucial to previously single, childless step-parents in particular. It is a loaded question, its outcome dependent on so many things. 'Ordinary' couples seem to have an easier choice to make, their decision to have a first child (or no children at all) being entirely their own affair. In a stepfamily, however, the deciding process is more complicated.

For a childless stepmother, it is very difficult. She already does have a family: her partner's. Does she want a child of her own? Can the family afford it? What about the case of an older man and a younger woman, she eager to have a child and he less so: either afraid of the new responsibility or simply reluctant to live through those early disruptive years all over again? She may feel that a child of the marriage would cement their relationship, whereas he may suspect that the advent of a baby would turn life neatly on its head. He could be frightened of losing an attractive attentive companion only to gain a mate more absorbed in the baby than in him. Quite apart from the emotional aspect, there is the practical one to consider. A woman could have her own well-paid job or be making real progress in her career: it could seem impossible to interrupt all that for a baby, however badly she may want one. There may not be enough money to go round if the woman gives up her job, or enough space in the existing house, with scant prospect of a move: a house already well filled with one family might not accommodate a baby as well.

If you're a stepmother wanting a child of her own, it can seem so unfair. Planned parenthood is very much the norm these days, with far less tolerance of the 'happy accident' of yesteryear. A woman in this situation could soon find that it is easier to give up. Her husband could be preoccupied with the demands of his own family (considering their ages and possible reactions, quite apart from anything else) and the financial implications of having a new infant; also, as if that's not enough, he may be worried about possible instability in his own job. In other words, there can be plenty of excuses to postpone talking about having a baby – sometimes indefinitely. Forgotten promises to discuss the subject productively and with realism result in disappointment: another short-cut to a tranquil life which can turn very sour. The worst possible thing anyone can do in these circumstances is make a deliberate 'mistake' resulting in an imminent but resented child. Change in partners' attitudes cannot, however, be ruled out. What happens, for instance, if the woman begins to go off the idea just as her man, starting to feel optimistic about his marriage and the existing family, suddenly gets unexpectedly broody? On the subject of whether or not to have a baby, I do feel that it is the childless partner who deserves priority. It is a decision which will affect him/her profoundly, making the difference between experiencing 'real' parenthood or never knowing it, problems and pleasures alike.

The pregnant stepmother whose decision-making stage is well and truly over could have many doubts about the new life to come. It is of course consoling to state that while there is no ideal moment for a baby to arrive in a stepfamily, ordinary families have this problem too. A woman might have reservations about actually caring for a baby once it is born, but she might be surprised at some of the benefits in store. A baby will never cure major ills either for a couple or a stepfamily, but it can turn what is a reasonably good situation into an excellent one. The stepchildren may be quite young, adolescent or grown up; their age matters little. In the forty short weeks that a pregnancy takes a family link will be born. How you use – or misuse – this link deserves careful thought.

If your stepchildren are with you part-time or just for holidays, it might be tempting to think that a baby won't really affect them. You are quite wrong. Your visitors might never admit this, but they can and will feel all the jealousy suffered by a toddler presented with a baby sister or brother. The small Babygro-clad being whisks away yet more parental attention, and should the older children be adolescents they won't express their fears and jealousies openly, as a toddler would.

Stepchildren who live permanently with you may join in the

initial congratulations on your pregnancy, but they'll be unconvinced. Everyone is excited about the baby, but what about *us*? Will we have to move bedrooms and possibly share (after having own bedrooms for a good while)? Are we going to be nobbled for babysitting – and if so, what about school work, which Dad always said was so important? Don't babies make a dreadful noise, especially in the middle of the night? Will we have to move? Will there be bottles and nappies all over the place, with both adults going 'gaga' over the infant all the time?

If you can reassure the children concerned that no one's bedroom will be annexed, then do so. If the family has to make changes, try to allow plenty of time and choice over them. Once the excitement has died down, put your pregnancy in the background. (This is admittedly impossible at, say, eight and a half months, but more than feasible early on.) A decidedly casual atmosphere all round might spawn a bit of interest in your condition, the occasional offer of help: shopping done for you, lifting jobs and so forth. But do bear in mind that this doesn't work if you declare yourself delicate as soon as you obtain a positive pregnancy test – unless, of course, you are specifically advised to rest.

If you sense that teenage girls and boys in your family are in any way embarrassed because Dad's got his new wife pregnant, then try to sympathize. They are at an age where sex is very much on the brain; convention dictates that growing adults prefer to forget their parents' sex life, especially if concentrating on their own. You growing pear-shape could prove a rather tactless reminder. If the family are still quite young, this could be a cure for the children to be reminded (or told) how babies materialize. Use your pregnancy to provide graphic information: they might feel a bit better if they know something about a developing baby.

So much for pregnancy. What about D-day and after? Unless you opt for a home birth, arrangements for a stay in hospital must be made, and as this is to be a crucial event in everyone's life it is as well to make them tactfully. After the birth of the baby, your partner is most needed by his own family, so it is worth his being at home if possible. Visits to hospital deserve mention here. Talk it over beforehand; ask your partner how he coped in the past, or refer to sections of well-written child care guides. The specially vulnerable stepchild, regardless of age, should not be treated to the tableau of mother, father and infant all huddled together and looking remarkably pleased with themselves; if this baby must be cuddled by anyone on this occasion, it might as well be you. Better still, why not encourage your stepchild to lift the infant out of its plastic hospital crib and take a good look at his/her new brother or sister – but perhaps not in a really crowded visiting hour where numerous relatives may flinch at seeing the inexperienced child ham-fistedly cuddling a day-old baby. The mention of relatives brings to mind something else of which you may not need reminding – but I intend to, anyway. Try at all costs to prevent anyone from passing tactless remarks to the effect that your stepchild is a 'half-brother' or a 'half-sister' to the new baby.

Someone might be silly enough to say something, unaware that this is no time for exact genealogical detail. You and your partner doubtless feel that the baby is a new brother or sister for all the family, so others should follow your lead.

Coming through the minefield of those early weeks with a baby may seem enough to handle, but again, a bit of mental preparation is worth while. Stepchildren may be prepared to see you in this strange occupation, and even have a go with the baby themselves; but it won't really help if Dad is seen cooing over the cradle at all times, praising the baby's negligible achievements just as if he'd never fathered a child in his life. If you are merely a threesome he can sound as daft as he likes, but here things will work better if he assumes a fairly casual manner in front of his older children. Again, unfair though it may seem to point the finger at friends and relatives, they too should be encouraged to 'cool it'. How would *you* feel, when asked for what seems the thousandth time that day: 'And what do you think of your little sister, then?' With the whole house gone mad, Dad completely distracted, loud crying breaking the silence every night and not a hot meal in sight for about a week, you the neglected stepchild could be sorely tempted to tell them *just* what you think!

So what happens once you've thought your way through pregnancy, got over the delivery and tried to ensure that the whole family isn't totally deprived of your or their dad's attention? You will be pleased to hear that the fun part starts here. This is when you suddenly realize that some of your stepchildren's irritating little ways just don't bother you any more. It is fun when they offer to help with a good heart, perhaps subjecting the infant to a very rough but loving bath and change of clothes. It is fun when they kiss and cuddle the new arrival and compete for the title of its favourite sister or brother. It is even fun when you are told, by a stepchild, with shattering honesty, that 'you're human now'.

You're human – big deal! But they're almost human, too. As long as stepchildren aren't made to feel excluded and therefore unwanted all the time the infant is either on the way or physically present, you will all share the new baby – and the family link will begin to work.

10

Talk About It!

Now you've read about some of the problems, and some of the pleasures, of step-parenthood. What happens next?

We hit another and rather strange problem: isolation. This is completely illogical, given the growing number of stepfamilies. I regularly glance up and down a suburban street mentally calculating the chances of a stepfamily inhabiting one of the neat houses. There could be hundreds somewhere among the thousands of households, some within yards of each other. Are all women and children seen at the shops or outside schools 'real' mums and kids – or are some of them stepmothers and stepchildren? And at work, how many people do you know by sight who could well be step-parents? Whenever there is an article in the press, a radio or TV broadcast (of which there aren't nearly enough) or a venture is started to put step-parents in touch, one hears the same comment time and again: 'Thank goodness! Someone else feels just like me!'

It will by now be apparent that one simple way round some of the stepfamily's problems is to talk about them. Discuss, if you can, whatever you don't understand or don't like very much or are afraid of. It matters little if the way you describe the situation isn't very articulate: today's slight misunderstanding becomes tomorrow's nagging problem, storing up more and more trouble the longer it's left. If there is something bothering one of the family today it will be far harder to discuss tomorrow, and the person concerned, already shy or hesitant, will have let the opportunity slip by: another short-term preserver of superficial peace and quiet which leads to long-term unhappiness. It is significant, in my view, that the Samaritans report a recent growth in the number of calls coming in from individuals with stepfamily-related problems. It is good to know that someone is on the end of a telephone – but it would be far better to think that those concerned did not have to ring and talk to a stranger.

Some topics can't easily be dealt with by family discussion.

Since there are almost as many kinds of stepfamily as there are circumstances which create them, I have deliberately refrained from including in this book chapters on law or finance. We accept that the role of step-parent brings with it many responsibilities but few rights, yet there are occasions when it is vital to sort out a financial wrangle, a problem arising from a parent's death which may leave the step-parent nominally in charge and so forth. Organizations such as the Citizens' Advice Bureaux and Ginger-bread may be of help here. In the case of a problem of a more personal nature which would benefit from outside counselling, it is worth contacting the Marriage Guidance Council, a body which is now taking a great interest in remarriage and stepfamilies.

Then of course, there is STEPFAMILY, our own association. Much hard work has been put in to crack the problem of stepfamilies' isolation through the use of telephone links, newsletters and meetings. If you see a group advertised locally, don't leave it to others – go along. It could be that you don't envisage talking about yourself in some cold, draughty hall, but from some very small groups larger ones grow. And if after some hard work in your own stepfamily you feel able to help someone else, try starting a group of your own. STEPFAMILY will be only too pleased to advise on what to avoid as well as on what to encourage.

Stepfamilies need to nourish their own self-confidence, and although our case is not yet hitting the headlines, this type of family structure, primarily of the eighties, is attracting increasing attention. When the general public get to know more about us, putting down their taboos once and for all, we can be optimistic of cracking the greater part of the isolation problem. Until then, we can't expect the fairy tales, often told with such ghoulish delight, to be rewritten. After all, the story of *Cinderella* would lose much of its impact if written like this: 'Once upon a time there was a little girl called Cinderella who lived in a big house with her father, who she loved very much, and a really nice stepmother and stepsisters who thought she was rather pretty, besides being good fun . . .'

If I thought that more people would shed some of their preconceived notions and fears about stepfamilies, I would not hesitate to rewrite *Cinderella* – even if it meant making the Good Fairy redundant!

Index